IT IS THE LORD!

Then the disciple whom Jesus loved said to Peter,
"It is the Lord!" (Jn 21:7)

IT IS THE LORD!

Sin and Confession Revisited

William J. Bausch

FIDES PUBLISHERS, INC.
NOTRE DAME   INDIANA

DOME edition   June 1970

© Copyright: 1970, Fides Publishers, Inc.
              Notre Dame, Indiana

Nihil Obstat: Louis J. Putz, C.S.C.
              University of Notre Dame

Imprimatur: Leo A. Pursley, D.D.
            Bishop of Fort Wayne-South Bend

Library of Congress Catalog Card Number: 72-104074

Standard Book Number: 8190-0552-5

CONTENTS

To Robert T. Bulman

PRIEST AND FRIEND

Introduction

For the past few years there has been occurring something of a minor phenomenon in the realm of confession. One measurable event is the general nation-wide falling off of the numbers of confessions. Those old long-lined Saturday nights are simply not there anymore. Then there's the not too measurable feeling that things aren't the same anymore either. Some people and priests are saying not to go to confession so much or that there's no such thing as mortal sin. Things that we thought were so terribly wrong ten years ago now seem positively virtuous. In some parishes they're not hearing children's confessions any longer and in fact are not even letting the kids go to confession before making their First Holy Communion. And this new communal confession business. We're not sure exactly what it is but it sounds too uncomfortably close to a kind of revival meeting where everyone stands up and shouts out his sins. Sounds like great fun as a spectator sport but not as a participant. And there is no indication that things are about to settle down. In fact, the Catholic has come across quotations from Vatican II declaring that "the rite and formulas for the Sacrament of Penance are to be revised so that they give a more luminous expression to both the nature and effect of the Sacrament." In a word, then, for the average Catholic, matters confessional are in a confusing state. This book is for him.

What does this book seek to do? It hopefully will answer all of the above issues. But this would only be a side-effect

1

for it really seeks something more, something deeper. This book seeks to shape attitudes. It seeks to explore better possibilities of making confession a joyous encounter. It seeks to lead the uninitiated away from the old mechanical "going to confession" to a renewed approach to a loving Person. If there is one focal point to this book, it is God; hence the book's title. From the first chapter on friendship to the last one on God's glory this book desires to free the Catholic penitent from any formula or fear that would inhibit his status as "son of God."

The author is only too acutely aware of the limitations of this book and asks the reader to acknowledge a similar awareness. For those who are more interested in deeper and more precise ideas and deeper theological ramifications a selected bibliography with notations is given at the end of this book in the appendix. I repeat, this book is limited. In fact, it is probably in order to say what it is *not* about. It is not a handbook of moral theology. It will not solve cases or engage in refined casuistry. It does not raise specific moral issues of the day and seek to answer them. There are other and more profound books that do this. Rather, this book is for the average Catholic who reads and who wonders about the questions I raised in the opening paragraph. It is meant to be a kind of introduction to fresh ideas on confession that will become more prominent as time goes on. It is meant to give him a personalist approach (although that word is nowhere used in this book) to confession. It is meant, finally, to shape up his own inner attitudes as he approaches the Lord with the common admission of us all, "O God, be merciful to me, a sinner!"

Toward all of these ends I have tried to keep this book simple and direct avoiding technicalities and controversies.

Even the sources of the frequent quotations have not been put in footnotes but, rather, included in the text. These quotations, moreover, were conscientiously chosen not only for their clarity in reference to the point at hand, but also to give indication to the reader that many important names are writing in depth in order to bring into proper perspective the great sacrament of reconciliation.

There are precious few if any original thoughts in this book. It contains, rather, the fruit of many writers and thinkers whose ideas I have assimilated to the extent that I no longer recall their source. I am grateful to the adults who have taken courses on this subject with me and have given me encouragement to put them down on paper. Finally I am indebted to Ann DeVizia who determinedly deciphered my notes and patiently typed the manuscript and to Sister Patricia Galvin, C.S.J., who provided the discussion questions as an aid to study groups.

I

Friendship

For the average Catholic picking up a book on sin and confession there is always the problem of hold-over concepts from the past. Sin itself, for example, is, in the last analysis, thought of in terms of quantity. It's a "thing" we do, a "thing" we incur. Yes, it's an "offense against God" but still it's a concrete offense and has meaning within itself alone. But with this concept, even though we define sin as an offense against God, we can leave God out of it entirely and spend our time on earth either trying to lessen the quantity or gaining grace—a comparison not unlike water being poured into a glass: the emptiness (sin) disappears as the liquid (grace) increases.

The "quantity" mentality spills over into our other relations with God. Our relationship, in fact, becomes a matching of wits: we trying to juggle enough credits to ward off the Almighty's recorded debits and in the end may the best mathematician win! How far can I go before mortal sin jells? how many indulgences can I gain to lessen the punishment due to sin? how close to Trinity Saturday dare I go before I can no longer make my Easter duty confession? how many venial sins add up to a mortal one? how many rules do I know to counter God's accusations?—all these questions are subconsciously or consciously quite preoccupying and misleading and all because our mental concept of sin as quantity has effectively led us to ignore the One Who really counts—Our Father in heaven.

In this chapter, therefore, we must start out fresh, we must put aside all of our former notions about sin and confession and repentance and begin with basic concepts of what in the world these things are really about anyway. Let's start with friendship.

What is friendship? We may define it as a special kind of love between two people, a kind of love that cares for another, shares with another and does for another and (most importantly) accepts another. Friendship is recognition, calling each other by name, sharing secrets and aspirations and knowing that in a pinch you can truly count on the other. Friendship is being comfortable with another; not weighing words every time so that even if you do say something outrageous or stupid or ignorant the other reads it for what it is—and doesn't laugh or call names. Friendship is staying at each other's homes, joining in vacations, calling one another in time of need and trusting each other and growing into old age known as friends. Friendship is all of these things and much more that can't be put into words.

But now we must make some observations and ask some questions about friendship. For example, an apparently fatuous question like "What *color* is friendship?" or "What's it smell like or taste like or feel like or sound like?" The answer is, of course, that friendship doesn't have a color or odor or feel or sound but—as most people would hasten to add—*it's real!* At least my friendship with Joe or Jane is real! True. But notice what you're saying: friendship is in effect invisible but real.

You see, we're so accustomed to think of as "real" only those things that are physical or tangible that we forget that as a matter of genuine fact most of the really real things in life *are* invisible: like truth, honesty—and love. Friendship is a special invisible but real love between two people. It's there, it exists, it's "felt," it's perceived even more than a car or dish towel. Who cannot look up from a hospital bed at the face of a friend and not know that the bond between you, although invisible, is more of a reality than the bed you're lying on? more satisfying, more comforting, more sustaining.

In her ever charming children's tale, *The Velveteen Rabbit*, Margery Williams describes the invisible reality of real.

> "What is Real?" asked the Rabbit one day when they were lying side by side near the nursery fender, before Nama came to tidy the room. "Does it mean having things that buzz inside you and a stick-out handle?"
>
> "Real isn't how you are made," said the Skin Horse. "It's a thing that happens to you. When a child loves you for a long, long time, not just to play with, but REALLY loves you, then you become REAL."
>
> "Does it hurt?" asked the Rabbit.
>
> "Sometimes," said the Skin Horse, for he was always truthful. "When you are Real you don't mind being hurt."
>
> "Does it happen all at once, like being wound up," he asked, "or bit by bit?"
>
> "It doesn't happen all at once," said the Skin Horse. "You become. It takes a long time. That's why it doesn't often happen to people who break easily, or have sharp edges, or who have to be carefully kept. Generally, by the time you are Real, most of your hair has been loved off, and your eyes drop out and you get loose in the joints and very shabby. But these things don't matter at all, because once you are

Real you can't be ugly, except to people who don't understand."

"I suppose *you* are Real?" said the Rabbit. And then he wished he had not said it, for he thought the Skin Horse might be sensitive. But the Skin Horse only smiled.

"The Boy's Uncle made me Real," he said. "That was a great many years ago; but once you are Real you can't become unreal again. It lasts for always."

In her winsome way the authoress is saying the first point of this chapter: the real things in life are the invisible but the truly valuable and transforming bonds and sentiments such as love and friendship and the like.

We have spent some time on this notion of friendship because all of our ups and downs in the course of friendship, our arguments and making up, derive from our grasp of what a friendship is. Now we must come to another friendship among the many we have. We must say quickly at first then more slowly, "God is our Friend."

I say quickly because that statement leaves us cold and indifferent at first; but if we say it slowly and remember all the things we've just said, then we can begin to realize that we really do have a relationship with a genuine Person and that this relationship is first and foremost one of friendship. Yes, there is a real but invisible bond between the heavenly Father and me. Moreover, this bond took on a special dimension when I was baptized because by baptism I became God's child and the name "Father" became a true reality. There is now, ever since, a special bond between us: Father and child, if you will; or Friend and friend.

Here is another huge mental hurdle for us: to think of God as a real Person capable of a real friendship. Alas, we've even managed to mechanize God. We've made a thing out of Him, kept Him in His heaven and have freed ourselves from dealing with Him on terms of love. As we said above, we've positioned ourselves and God into mutually distrusting bargaining sides in a game of moral checkers: we trying to be shrewd enough to get crowned king and God trying to outwit us to prevent such a disaster.

Yet, God is our Friend and Father. There is a special bond between us and thus a special friendship. We have a name for this friendship between God and His creature and, again, there is a reluctance to use the term because it has too become mathematized with age: it is "grace." How this word, like sin, has become a word of quantity! a thing! I must "gain grace" or increase it or what have you. People will approach the sacraments like a car approaching a filling station. "Five gallons of grace, please!" But no, grace is that mysterious bond between a Friend—who is really too high to be a friend to mere mortals—and us. We *can* grow in grace but like we grow in friendship. There's no increase of quantity but rather a deepening of quality. There's another word, anyway, that should probably be better used instead of grace for the next fifty years and that is "the Indwelling." The "Indwelling" connotes the more personal truth of intimacy, a real "dwelling-in" of God within the heart of a friend. And God is so capable of doing this. In the Old Testament He showed Moses that He was his friend and (like all good friends) knew his name:

> Yahweh would speak with Moses face to face, as a man speaks with his friend . . . Yahweh said to Moses, "Again I will do what you have asked because you have won my favor and because I know you by name" (Ex 33:11, 17).

Christ mentioned this special friendship of "Indwelling" in the New Testament:

> "Because I live, you too will live; then you will know that I am in my Father and you in me and I in you.
>
> "Anyone who loves me will heed what I say; then my Father will love him and we will come and make our dwelling with him" (Jn 14:23).

St. Paul exclaimed, "Do you realize that you are Temples of God who lives in you?"

Yes, there is a genuine friendship between the Father and us. A real but invisible bond that is the substance of our lives and makes us more Real. A genuine love between genuine persons. Let us look further into this friendship-love. It is relevant here to repeat St. John's platitude that it was God who first loved us. God was the Initiator, the one who made the first gesture of love, who extended the hand of friendship. For those people who have always experienced the acceptance and love of their parents from the very beginning, this is a great mystery but somehow within the grasp of the heart. Early experience of human love makes the mystery of God's love delightfully real. For those unfortunate people who have not experienced human love, the mystery of God's love is forbidding and suspect. It will take a mighty effort to jump to accepting the thrust of God's love without a human foundation. But for all adults, whatever their early experience, the friendship-love of God is there and is measurable. One of Elisabeth Barrett Browning's famous sonnets begins "How do I love thee? Let me count the ways." Let us here briefly count some of the ways that the warm and personal love of the Father has extended itself to us to make us friends forever.

God loves us by creating us. He could have created others and could have created them better than ourselves, holier, nobler—but He did not. There was something about us alone that was different. Some quality that only we would have. He passed over others to make us. It's like a bride and groom planning to build a house. They look through the catalogue and bypass many plans. Finally they exclaim together, "Wait, here's the house we like. It's just what we've always dreamed of! Let's build it." The couple leave unbuilt all of the other houses to build the one of their choice. So it was with God. There are many men and women, boys and girls not here on earth. They were not created. But we were. We have been chosen. To be chosen is to be wanted. To be wanted is to be loved. God loves us by creating us.

God loves us by providing. He gave us parents, a home, faith, the special link of baptism. He snatches dangers from our paths and gives us constantly opportunities to learn of Him. He has placed us, for our sakes, at the right moment of history at the right place. He has arranged everything—even our hardships—in order that we might grow into a good human being and into a saint.

God loves us by telling us so. Like any shameless lover. He tells us He loves us. Outright. Through the Prophet Jeremiah He says, "Tell the people, Behold I have loved you with an everlasting love!" Through Isaiah He asks, "Can a mother forget the child of her womb? Even if she should forget, I will not forget you." St. John says in his gospel, "The Father so loved the world that He sent His only begotten son." In short, the valentines from God are both numerous and touching.

God loves us by pursuing us. *That* truly is an embarrassment! God running after us. But He does. The great christian apologist C. S. Lewis reminds us that God stoops to conquer, that even when we have tried everything and everybody but Him and now come crawling to Him simply because we have no place to go, He will still take us back. *We* wouldn't do that; we have too much pride. But not God. He really does stoop to conquer. Like the Hound of Heaven that Francis Thompson made Him out to be He pursues us—what is that but love?

Finally, we may pause over the most compelling proof of God's love. God loves us by becoming us. Perhaps His majesty was too frightening, perhaps in spite of all the other proofs of His love, there was too large of a gap for our human fears to bridge, perhaps heaven and earth were simply too wide apart for us to really think of a loving God. In any case, as any real lover, God could not tolerate separation, even in our minds, so He became one of us. He became like us, says St. Paul, in all things but sin. Now we had a God who knew the human experience, who took on the limitations of mortal flesh, who knew what it was to sweat, to bleed and to suffer a broken human heart. Now we had "Emmanuel"—God with us, Jesus Christ. Jesus is the concretized love of God for man. Jesus is walking, talking friendship. Jesus is the in-the-flesh union of God and man. Jesus is God's love. And as God's love it was He who proceeded to tell us the story of the prodigal son and how forgiving God is. He told us of the lost sheep and how God is like a good shepherd who goes to look for it. He told us about how kind God is who makes it rain on the good and the evil, who counts every hair in our heads, who gives us our daily bread. Who sees what we do in secret and rewards it, who knows everything that we need.

All this, everything we have pointed out in this chapter, holds up one fact before our eyes: God loves us and as a personal, genuine lover He has extended that love to us in friendship. And, as we shall see in the next chapter, friendship—that real but invisible bond between persons—is the basis for understanding sin and repentance.

II

Sin

1

The only way one can really know what a crooked line is, is to know what a straight line is. Sickness is known only in reference to health. There must be some standard, in other words, before a defect can be recognized and known. This is why we spent the first chapter on friendship. Only when the reality of friendship becomes a part of our consciousness can we know what it means to deviate from that friendship.

Have you ever had an argument with your friend? Gotten angry with him? Has your friend ever said or done things that have hurt you? Have you ever experienced one of life's greatest losses, that of a broken friendship? Anger and argumentation are bad and they often hurt feelings. People wind up saying and doing things they really don't mean and before they know it, a great friendship has been wounded or destroyed. At party time someone is looking over the guest list and remarks, "Where's Mary? Aren't you inviting Mary? She's your best friend!" The reply is, "Oh, well—she and I had a few words over some silly thing. In fact, we had a rather nasty fight. We're not friends any more." And there is sadness here, a sadness that a good friendship was broken, no longer exists.

But again notice that this reality too is invisible. I mean, that just as you could not get at your essential friendship with any of your five senses, could not see or feel it, yet you know it was there and real—so, too, is the destruction of that friendship invisible and, alas, real. In other words, the broken friendship is nothing you can see; it's not a physically broken object that you can put on display for everyone to observe, but there's an emptiness, a feeling in the heart, a terrible absence. The invisible but real friendship no longer is there. You can't put your finger on it (literally) but you *know* something's happened, something's wrong. The "something's wrong" is not measurable by any physical rule but truly perceived by the spirit, admitted in the mind and felt in the heart. Of course, as was indicated above, only one who has experienced friendship is capable of knowing its opposite, is capable of encountering a wounded or broken friendship.

This, once more, is why the first chapter was on God's friendship with us. Only when we can truly accept this fact, can the awful reality of breaking that friendship with Him be appreciated and understood. Because we are dealing with someone unique and so powerful we try to use separate words to heighten what we know among ourselves. For example, we used the words "grace" or "Indwelling" to speak of our special bond of baptism-friendship with God. So, too, we have a special word for wounding or breaking that friendship with the Almighty: it is sin.

Sin is either hurting or breaking our friendship with God. I know that for some this definition is not quite satsfactory. Perhaps the old concept of a big black "mark" on the soul was more comforting; at least it was more concrete, more "located." But sin isn't physical any more than are love and truth and friendship or unlove and falsehood and broken friendship—all are matters of the spirit. They show themselves in physical ways, but are in essence spiritual realities.

The old concept of sin as a physical "mark" or a *thing* we do or omit has far-reaching drawbacks on one's spiritual life. For one thing it leads to a "taboo" mentality; that is, we do or avoid certain things because they of themselves make us good or bad. When we "sin" in this sense, then repentance means using some countermoves, such as gaining indulgences or getting absolution in confession or performing certain actions to take away the sin. Under this system it is possible to commit sin and obtain forgiveness without once referring to God! Sin and repentance become that battle of moral checkers we mentioned before: trying to maneuver God into forgiveness provided you know the correct formulas or actions that will force His hand.

But if sin is seen as a friendship wounded or broken, then we are dealing with persons: ourselves and God. Then we are forced to look at the sides: the magnificent and loving Father on the one side, the small and ungrateful child on the other. Then repentance becomes a personal involvement, a reaching out to a someone, a falling before a Father, a grasping of a person. It's awfully hard to be sorry for offending a 'system'; it's still more difficult to be reconciled to a corporation. But there is no trouble at all in realizing that an offense against a real person and reconciliation with a real person is an approach any man can make.

This should be obvious but it is not. We are so used to being impersonal with the Father that we cannot grasp the reality of His personhood and the reality of His friendship. Still less, therefore, can we grasp the reality of sin: a wounded or broken friendship with a friend.

"But that seems so—vague!" you may say. True, but no vaguer than any wounded or broken friendship. When you and your friend do quarrel or even break up, there are no visible evidences of this. In fact, if you're a good enough actor no one may ever know the heaviness of your heart over this affair. But you know. And he or she knows. You can't put your or anyone else's finger on it, but something *real* has happened. You *know* you've done something against your friend and things are not just the same anymore. The broken friendship is not a measured commodity, but an inner, real absence. Sin is precisely that. Take any wounded or broken friendship with a human being, apply the same case to God and you have sin.

As with human beings, there are degrees of hurt. Applied to God in the technical language of the theologians these degrees are called "venial" and "grave" (though this distinction came in centuries later in christianity). Venial sin might be described as that which disturbs or annoys the friendship with God, but does not destroy it in any profound way. It's like the little things you might do to your friends: they are annoying but do not basically hurt or injure the friendship. In any real friendship, of course, even these annoyances must be avoided because if you truly love someone you will never try to bother them or disturb them or do anything that would lessen the depth of your love. Rather, you always strive to build up that love. This is why Protestants are generally impatient with the Catholic distinction between venial and grave sin. They feel that if you really do love God, *any* sin— no matter how minor—is unworthy of the majestic friendship of God and we shouldn't really measure higher and lower cases of sin when it comes to Him. In any case, this distinction, while valuable, has had some ill side effects on Catholics. It has, in some cases, produced the "slide-rule mentality": how far can I go without committing a grave sin? "This is all right, it's only a venial sin!" The motivation, in other words, is not worrying about love itself, about the "I-Thou" relationship, but about the mathematical precision of just how far you can go before you really stop liking each other. It's like a husband seeing just how far he can cheat on his wife and abuse her and at the same time keep her out of the divorce court. If he really loves her, he won't think of measuring his abuse; true love will urge him not to even consciously give the slightest hurt. We fall into the same mentality. "It's just a venial sin" is like saying, "I'm only hurting my friendship with God a little bit!" Yet Cardinal Newman wrote that a venial sin is a greater metaphysical evil than a global catastrophe that would bring death to millions.

The other general category of sin is grave sin. Often this is erroneously called "Mortal Sin"; but mortal sin is so special a thing, so precise a state that we will avoid this term here and explain it later on. Grave sin, as its name indicates, really hurts the God-man friendship in a serious way. Here is no mere annoyance, but a genuine blow. Oh, the friendship is still open to repair. There hasn't been a final, irrevocable and permanent breaking off, but, nevertheless, a serious hurt has been given and received. This is the grave sin that, for Catholics, requires confession. Venial sin can be forgiven outside of confession.

Perhaps the difference between grave and venial sin can be taken from words used by Jesus Himself. He said, "If any

man loves me, my Father will love him and we will come
and take our dwelling with him." Actually, in the original
Hebrew Jesus is saying literally something His hearers (who
were used to sleeping outdoors) could really understand.
He really expressed Himself this way: "If any man loves me
. . . we will come and pitch our tent with him." Yes, God the
Father, God the Son and God the Holy Spirit pitch their tent
within a person in the state of "grace" or the state of abiding
personal friendship. Venial sin may be likened to God kind
of rattling together the pots and pans. He's plainly uncom-
fortable and not altogether at home although He's staying
put. Grave sin may be likened to God's folding up the tent
altogether and moving on. He doesn't move too far away and
He's open for a return; in fact, He's left two tent ropes there
(faith and hope) so you can pull Him back when you have
a mind to. Indeed, He is most anxious for a renewal of friendship, for apology and reconciliation, most anxious to re-pitch
His tent within you. But you've offended Him seriously and
He simply cannot stay while you show that you not only do
not love Him but actually prefer something else or someone
else to Him.

Viewing grave and venial sins in this light may seem sim-
plistic, but this view is accurate. More. It is superior to viewing sin of any kind as a "mark" or "spot" on the soul, something incurred almost accidentally and gotten rid of by legal
gymnastics. As we said at the beginning, one can only know
what a crooked line is if he knows what a straight line is. So,
too, one can only begin to fathom the enormity of sin when
one has felt the impress of a personal friendship with a God
who calls himself Father. The friendship is invisible but real;
a wounded or broken friendship is invisible but real. Repentance must take this into account and be approached pri-

marily on the personal level. The restoration must be in the heart. Any outward signs must demonstrate an inner repair of the existential friendship between God and man.

2

A further question about sin is in order: what are its conditions? To answer this let us draw once more on our own human experiences. Your friend is angry with you because you gave her magazine to someone else. Actually you thought she was finished with it and didn't want it anymore. She read it, tossed it aside and that was that. When someone else was looking for something to read you generously gave her your friend's magazine. As it turned out, she *wasn't* finished with it and is quite annoyed that you gave her magazine away. When she scolds you for this, what is the first thing you say? You exclaim, "But I didn't do it on purpose! I thought you were finished reading it!" Deep down you feel hurt that your friend is angry over a mistake. Doesn't she understand that you didn't *mean* to do it? In other words, although you did wrong in giving the magazine away, you're not guilty for it.

This example embodies the three elements necessary to break or wound any friendship. In reference to our Father, it provides the three elements to commit sin. First, is knowledge. One must know what one is doing—and know it as wrong. Secondly, one must give full and final consent and thirdly, the matter at hand must be wrong. All three ingredients must go together in order to have a sin. This summary is something we all learned as children, but we somehow dropped one or two elements, somehow got stuck on a false emphasis and the resulting mischief still works havoc among us. Thus:

"Bless me Father, I have sinned. It is one month since my last confession. I missed Mass twice."

"Did you miss Mass through your own fault or was there some good reason why you couldn't come?"

"Well, you see, I was sick and in the hospital and couldn't go."

"But if you were sick, you didn't need to go. There is no sin here."

"I know, Father, but I feel better if I mention it."

That "feeling better" is a slight case of moral schizophrenia which is not uncommon. But notice here. One of the essential ingredients for sin was missing in this case: consent. She didn't want to miss Mass; she knew she was missing it, but she couldn't help it. Without consent, how could there be sin? There could be "wrong-doing" if you will; that is, the act of missing Mass in itself was not right, but sin? how could there be? Yet this penitent and perhaps thousands of others continue to confess as sins what are in fact not sins at all.

Let me put it another way. Not every wrong-doing is necessarily a sin. A wrong doing stands on its own feet and as such is bad; but we never, never conclude it is sin until—and only until—we look to the person committing the wrong-doing. Sin is the product of the wrong doing *plus* the person's knowledge and consent. Thus killing is a wrong-doing. Is it a sin? Yes and no. If there was knowledge and consent, there is sin. If there was neither—for example, the subject was sleep-walking when he perpetrated the murder—then there was wrong-doing, but certainly no sin.

Wrong-doing is a mechanical product. Sin is a human product. You must have the person involved before there is a question of sin. To have it any other way would be to make God a terrible monster who sets up mechanical taboos in order to catch His subjects in the wrong. Our trouble is that people do judge on the outside, and many times they are wrong. How often have you been caught in an act or word that looked or sounded guilty but in fact you were perfectly innocent? Remember how frustrated you became that it really wasn't the way it looked or sounded? Although you looked guilty you were innocent.

The psalmist explains this situation by saying, "Man looks at the face, God looks at the heart." This is eminently true. As a friend who sees into our hearts, God never judges us by our wrong doings; that is, things we do on the outside, but rather by what we understand and want inside. This works both ways. Good deeds on the outside without a corresponding love on the inside are worthless. In other words, God believes in a morality of the heart and this is the basis for our technical division of the threefold ingredients necessary for sin. Jesus put the "inside-related-to-the-outside" this way:

> "You have learnt how it was said, 'You must not kill' . . . But I say to you: anyone who is angry with his brother will answer for it before the court. . . ."

> "Be careful not to parade your good deeds before men to attract their notice . . . your almsgiving must be secret and your Father who sees all that is done in secret will reward you."

> "When you fast, put oil on your head and wash your faces so that no one will know you are fasting except your Father who sees all that is done in secret. . . ."

Once more, to break or wound one's friendship with God, to sin, three simultaneous elements must be present much like three angles must be simultaneously present in order to have a triangle. There must be the wrong doing, there must be knowledge that this is wrong (even though one's knowledge is erroneous) and there must be consent. Any other approach is to consort with magic and taboo and superstition. People who commit sin "by accident" are victims of taboo. People who confess wrong-doings as sins are victims of superstition; people who try to elicit from the priest by hook or crook absolution are victims of magic. Father Rahner expresses his comments on this matter:

Who has not innumerable times experienced confessions which are simply rattled off, which go simply through the catalogue of sins mechanically? Every priest has experienced confessions where underneath a personally and perhaps quite innocent but terribly legalistic and magical atttiude, the only thing that seems to matter is the sacramental event as such; confessions in which, if necessary, sins are invented so that there may be something to confess; confessions in which objective sins [wrong-doing] are treated in exactly the same way as subjective sins [real sins]; confessions where the person believes that one should confess, for instance, having missed Mass even though one had been ill in bed and could not go to Mass; confession where the person believes he is making a good confession, even though he is out to pull the wool over the confessor's eyes or to confess when there is as much noise in the church as possible. . . . Who has not at some time instructed penitents about a fact that something is not a sin at all, and then has nevertheless been given the impression that this does not make the penitent feel relieved but that he would rather confess the same thing again? How often do people confess "just in case," so that God will not have anything "on us," and as if one had to or could insure oneself against Him, as though God could debit one with something when we ourselves did not recognize any clear duty? (*Theological Investigations*, vol. III, p. 195, 196)

All of this is again a way of saying that if you want to wound or break your friendship with God, you've got to know what you're doing. God is simply too big and too noble to be offended by the accidents or unthinking blunders in our lives. If our own parents will smile at our unpremeditated accidents, why not our heavenly Father? If love requires my personal touch, why not unlove or sin? If friendship calls for my personal and conscious participation, why not any alteration of that friendship? Sin is not the outcome of automatic, mechanized deeds; it is the result of a knowing and consenting hurt to a person. It is, for example, this precise sense of person-to-person that led David to cry out after his sin, "Against you only have I sinned!"

3

David's remark here brings up one final point of this chapter: if sin is basically a wounding or breaking of a grace-friendship with the Father and repentance is a patching up of this same friendship, then it becomes obvious that, at least on our part, a healthy *sense of sin* is the beginning of salvation. Only when one has realized his fault, accepts responsibility for it and repents can one grow as a human being. Honest self-awareness of being a sinner is the start. Nietzsche wrote, "An uneasy conscience is a sickness; but it is a sickness akin to pregnancy." In other words, as Arnold Uleyn comments in his book, *Is It I, Lord?*, an uneasy conscience is akin to pregnancy "because it bears within it the seed of a new life" (p. 23). Cases of excessive and enervating guilt do not negate the need for man to realize that he is a sinner; that it was he and none other who perpetrated the breakdown of the divine friendship and that it is he and none other who must approach his friend humbly and ask for pardon. Destructive guilt will lead to despair and, in the last analysis, is blasphemy because the sinner is declaring that God is not God—that is, He either cannot or will not forgive. Worse still, such a sinner says in reality that God doesn't love him, and not to believe that God loves one surely must be the unforgivable sin. F. J. Heggen in his excellent book, *Confession and the Service of Penance*, remarks, "Thus the New Testament often speaks of sin as unbelief. This is essentially the same thing as not allowing oneself to be helped, to be loved. Unbelief is the refusal to entrust oneself to Him who reveals himself in Jesus."

Perhaps the two prototypes of destructive and constructive guilt are Judas and Peter. As Father Joseph Manton reminds us, both apostles committed the same sin of betrayal. Judas sold Christ and Peter declared "I know not the man!" Both felt compunction. Judas went even one better than Peter: he was willing to return his ill-gotten money. Yet today we honor St. Peter and know not Judas' fate because Judas' guilt was destructive, self-pitying and essentially an unbelieving state that would not allow him to realize that Jesus loved him so much that his sin was nothing compared to the magnitude of that love. Peter, on the other hand, had constructive guilt: it led him back to his only refuge and hope— Jesus himself.

As always, Father Evely states the case beautifully in *We Dare To Say Our Father* when he says:

Religion consists in those wonders of generosity, love and forgiveness which God does for us. . . . God is so good that it is He who comes to us, who searches for us, who gives himself to us, who loves us. . . . We continually forget that we are not Christians because we love God; we are Christians because we believe that God loves us. . . .

. . . The essential thing is not no longer to sin, but to love, to have learnt His love. You will go to heaven because you will be pleased with God and not because you are pleased with yourself . . .

We complicate things to such an extent that we forget *the* condition without which all confessions would be farcical: to believe that God loves us. . . .

All this presupposes one essential fact for the human being: he must acknowledge his sinfulness and tie it in with faith, hope and love. Pascal said, "Man's knowledge of God without an awareness of his own wretchedness leads to pride. An awareness of his wretchedness without the knowledge of God leads to despair. The knowledge of Jesus Christ represents the middle state because we find in it both God and our wretchedness."

Thus in summary we have friendship: whole, wounded or broken. Man himself refuses to make his friendship with God grow and thus commits sin. Sin is the God-man friendship wounded or broken. It is done with knowledge and consent. Under the Spirit of God man must come back to His Father. He must renew in this day and age a sense of sin and constructive guilt. Once more modern man must learn to cry out with the Psalmist:

Happy the man whose fault is forgiven,
whose sin is blotted out;

happy the man whom Yahweh
accuses of no guilt,
whose spirit is incapable of deceit!
All the time I kept silent, my bones were wasting away
with groans, day in, day out;
day and night your hand
lay heavy on me;
my heart grew parched as stubble
in summer drought.
At last I admitted to you I had sinned;
no longer concealing my guilt,
I said, "I will go to Yahweh
and confess my fault."
And you, you have forgiven the wrong I did,
have pardoned my sin. (psalm 32)

If modern man does not pray this prayer then he lives under
a most dangerous illusion and comes under the chastisement
of the Apostle John's words, "If we say we have no sin in us,
we are deceiving ourselves and refusing to admit the truth;
but if we acknowledge our sins, then God who is faithful
and just will forgive our sins and purify us from everything
that is wrong. To say that we never have sinned is to call
God a lair and to show that His word is not in us" (Jn 1:
8-10).

III

Christian Morality

1

In the last chapter we have seen something of sin's definition and its conditions. We emphasized again that sin must be viewed in personal terms and must be a real interaction of Person-to-person. In this chapter we must look at just what that Person with a capital "P" considers as sin. Maybe He and we have not the same notions of what makes right and wrong, of what might possibly wound or break our friendship. So we must ask. We must listen.

To listen to God about what He has to say about the conditions of our friendship is to listen to Jesus. Jesus is God in the flesh; He is God speaking, teaching, guiding. Jesus is God with a human voice. He is God's love concretized. He is not only that love in human dimensions, but Jesus is the messenger who teaches us how to love God, how to increase and mature in His friendship. In His own words He is "the way, the truth and the life." The sum total of Jesus' teaching on building up our friendship with the Father is called christian morality.

When Jesus taught us about morality He didn't line up exact and precise rules. This is not to say His teaching is fuzzy, but to say that He gave us principles rather than applications; He gave us norms that are clear but that leave a lot up to the inner spirit of responding to these norms. In general, as Father Curran reminds us in his book, *A New Look at Christian Morality*, Jesus' morality was based on two assumptions: first, there is such a bond between loving God and loving our neighbor that one is dependent on the other. Jesus' own criterion for getting to heaven is given in Matthew 25: feeding the hungry, visiting the sick, etc., winding up with the conclusion that "as long as you did it to one of these, the least of my brethren, you did it to me." Later on St. John puts the case more bluntly by telling us that if we say we love God yet do not love our neighbor, we are liars. Secondly, there is the universality of just who is our neighbor upon whose loving depends the love of God. The answer is, Everyman, anyone, the foreigner called the Good Samaritan. Love, then, is the basis of Jesus' teaching. So pervasive is this love ethic that some have either concluded that Jesus was an impossible idealist or have simply retreated to one side of the question. Catholics, for example, have tried to resolve the question of Jesus' total lovingness by relegating this way of perfection to the clergy and religious and having the laity retreat to a kind of sub-standard Christianity of rule-keeping. So impossible was it to follow the teaching of Christ that it was left to people who professionally could give time to it. The result has been not only an unhealthy emphasis on the legal minimum for the laity, but the almost total loss of the development of an invigorating spirituality for the layman.

What, basically, is the principle that Jesus gave us to go by? It is something we've seen in the previous chapter: interior purity of intention. Another way of saying this is that in all of our approaches with God and man we must try as best we can sincerely to love and to mean that love inside. The place of the Ten Commandments in the system of Jesus is to act as a minimal guide. We are, of course, to keep the Ten Commandments, but we can't run our lives just on them alone. Beyond the Commandments there is a whole range of spirit and love-thrust that will carry them to new heights. Beyond the literal words of the Commandments, according to Jesus, are all sorts of avenues of charity which His follower is bound to travel.

This extension of Jesus was vigorously proposed by his fiery disciple, St. Paul who had a constant struggle with the Jews of his time to get them beyond the mere minimum and legalism of the Commandments. In their book, aptly entitled *Beyond the Commandments*, authors Killgallon and Weber explain:

> There are Catholics today who expect an external guideline such as the law was in the Old Testament. They want to be told what to do and what not to do. They take as their norm of perfection the Ten Commandments, and they are forever trying to apply them to their daily lives. These people do not understand the meaning of the Christian life. Theirs is essentially an Old Testament morality. They have not really grasped the message of Christ. They have not heard the words of St. Paul, "Before the faith came we were kept imprisoned under the Law, shut up for the faith that was to be revealed. Therefore the Law has been our tutor in Christ, that we might be justified by faith. But now that faith has come, we are no longer under a tutor. For you are all the children of God through faith in Jesus Christ. For all you who have been baptized into Christ have put on Christ. . . . *For if you are led by the Spirit you are not under the Law*" (Gal 3:23; 5:18).

St. Paul says that Christians are not "under the law." Is he, then, saying that Christians do not have to keep the Ten Commandments? Obviously not. Common sense would tell us that. What, then, does he mean by saying that Christians are no longer "under the law"?

Actually, what St. Paul is saying is that, while Christians must observe the Ten Commandments—as did the Jews, as must all men—the Christian life is not circumscribed by the Ten Commandments. He is saying that the norm of morality for the Christian is not the Ten Commandments, but something beyond. He is saying that the Christian is bound to God not by a law, as were the Jews, but by a Person, Jesus Christ. He is saying that, while the Christian observes all the precepts of the basic moral law, he looks for guidance and inspiration not to that law, but to the Holy Spirit dwelling within him and fashioning him in the image of Christ.

In short, what St. Paul is saying is that what is expected of the Christian is Christian maturity, a maturity which could never have been achieved nor even expected under the Old Law, before the coming of Christ.

An example of this maturity was Jesus' attitude towards the fifth Commandment, "Thou shalt not kill." He told us that that was only an outside limit and that a person cannot declare himself to be a real Christian if all that he can say is "I haven't killed anyone." Maybe he's been angry and unkind in his speech about another, called him "fool" and has a killing hatred in his heart for his brother. True, this man has not literally committed murder but neither has he loved and so he has sinned. And again, so tied in is this love of neighbor with the love of God that the two are inseparable and the one must be reformed before friendship with God can possibly grow. Jesus put it this way:

> If when you are bringing your gift to the altar you suddenly remember that your brother has a grievance against you, leave your gift where it is before the altar. First go and make your peace with your brother, and only then come back and offer your gift.

You see, interior intention, love in the heart is all important and is our human challenge. That's why we mentioned before and will explain again that sin cannot be measured by the outward act itself. We must look to the person before we can say of any wrong-doing "This is a sin." External acts alone do not make a man holy or unholy. Thus, Jesus' scolding of the Pharisees:

> "When you do an act of charity, do not announce it with a flourish of trumpets, as the hypocrites do in the synagogue and in the streets to win admiration from men . . . No; when you do some act of charity . . . your good deed must be secret and your Father who sees what is done in secret will reward you." (Matt 6:3)

This is why Jesus threw up to the Pharisees their talent for being so scrupulous about paying all of the minor religious offerings but overlooking "the weightier demands of the Law; justice, mercy and good faith"; for taking great care to clean the outside of the cup and dish but are filled inside "by robbery and self-indulgence"; for looking well from the outside, appearing to be honest men, but inside "you are brim-full of hypocrisy and crime!" (Matt 23:23). It's an intention of the heart that forms the basis of Jesus' teaching on right and wrong. F. J. Heggen puts the matter well. This somewhat lengthy quotation from his book, *Confession and the Service of Penance*, bears close reading:

> That which we meet in scripture we also discover once more in our own lives. Beneath all the external identity between

two acts an enormous difference in meaning can be present. Two people can do precisely the same thing, whilst it is *not* the same thing in each case. We partially express this insight in the words we use. Killing someone and murdering them is not the same thing. It *is* something entirely different, even though this difference need not be visible in the outward activity which realizes the event. Saying something which is not true is not always a case of lying. A kiss can be the expression of sympathy or love, but it can also be the sign of the traitor. And without wishing to pass judgement in the question of marital relations, we may say that every concrete method of birth-regulation can be motivated by egoism and shortsightedness, but also by real concern for family and marriage partner. Even here no method is simply good or simply bad. Outwardly the same operation, the removal of a healthy kidney, can in one case be an aimless mutilation and in another—that of transplantation—a deed of love and human fellowship *par excellence*.

Far too little attention is paid to this fact, at least in the practice of moral judgment. Here "measuring up the act as it stands," establishing with a photographic objectivity "what is taking place" has had and continues to have clear priority over the question "what is this person really trying to do?", "what is the significance of his action?", "what does it mean in the context of his life, with its past and its future?", "what does it mean for others; does it build up or disrupt the community?" We must constantly bear in mind that our human activity is essentially intersubjective. Furthermore, we may not cut this activity up into small pieces so as to then study each piece separately, making abstraction, moreover, of the living intention of the person acting. . . .

. . . We are now perhaps in a better position to understand the reaction of Jesus to the Pharisees' blind adhesion to the law and overestimation of works, as also to the sinfulness of so many of the poor in spirit. An essential element of conversion and thus of repentance can now help us to see the problem more clearly.

When the Lord denounces the piety of the Pharisees his rejection is not of real piety but of its inauthentic practice, of the false attitude which factually underlies it. It is he who sees into the heart of man; the intention which can remain hidden for us external spectators now becomes manifest. "Previously it had not yet been known what was hiding beneath that upper layer of an awareness in which sin and conversion took place. It was not generally known that underneath there slumbered a self-satisfaction, attachment to which attached one to sin."

Christ saw through the external facade. He saw what a person was really doing, searching for, and trying to manifest in his life. For this reason his judgment was—and is—often so different from that of those who wield an external criterion, which they call objective. According to the Gospel of John, people were divided around Jesus, the Light and Life of the world, into those who believed and those who refused to do so. A division takes place, but it is a division which consists of a process of crystalization around Christ.

Henceforth we know that God does not judge us on outward behavior, but on what goes on in our heart.

All right, since Jesus' morality is one of inside sincerity to match outside practice, what must His follower do? How must he act? The answer is he must constantly purify his intentions and give service. Thus:

- he must have concern and compassion for his fellow man—even one not of his personal liking:

  "Go and do likewise" Jesus said after telling the story of the Good Samaritan.

- he must love even his enemies:
  "Do not set yourself against a man who wrongs you" (Matt 5:39).
- he must pray:
  "When you pray, say, 'Our Father . . .'"
- he must share:
  "He who has two cloaks give one . . ."
- he must not judge the inner motives of another:
  "Judge not and you will not be judged."
- he must love every man:
  "By this all men will know that you are my disciples if you have love for one another."
- he must practice the corporal and spiritual works of mercy:
  "As long as you did it to these, the least of my brethren you did it to me" (Matt 25).
- he must be good to the poor:
  Luke 16:19.
- he must be merciful and forgiving:
  "Even if your brother wrongs you seven times in a day and comes back to you seven times saying 'I am sorry,' you are to forgive him" (Luke 17:4).
- he must be open to the invitations of God:
  Luke 14:15ff.
- he must risk all for the kingdom of God:
  Matthew 25:14-30.

Perhaps at this point, lest we get dismayed at these high ideals, we should listen to the complaint of St. Paul—and to his answer:

I am a thing of flesh and blood, sold into the slavery of sin. Of this I am certain, that no principle of good dwells in me, that is, in my natural self; praiseworthy intentions are always ready to hand, but I cannot find my way to the performance of them. Inwardly I applaud God's disposition, but I observe another disposition in my lower self, which raises war against the disposition of my conscience, and so I am handed over as a captive to that disposition towards sin which my lower self contains. Pitiable creature that I am, who is to set me free from a nature thus doomed to death? Nothing else than the grace of God, through Jesus Christ our Lord (Rom 7:14).

2

We've made several references and quotations concerning Jesus' exasperation with the legalism of the Pharisees. Let's put them all together and draw further conclusions:

Alas for you, scribes and Pharisees, you hypocrites! You who shut up the kingdom of heaven in men's faces, neither going in yourselves nor allowing others to go in who want to.

Alas for you, scribes and Pharisees, you hypocrites! You who travel over sea and land to make a single convert, and when you have him you make him twice as fit for hell as you are.

Alas for you, scribes and Pharisees, you hypocrites! You who pay you tithe of mint and dill and cummin and have neglected the weightier matters of the Law—justice, mercy, good faith! These they should have practiced without neglecting the others. You blind guides! Straining out gnats and swallowing camels!

Alas for you, scribes and Pharisees, you hypocrites! You who clean the outside of cup and dish and leave the inside full of extortion and imtemperance. Blind Pharisee! Clean the inside of the cup and dish first so that the outside may become clean as well (Matt 23:13ff).

With many other words did Jesus lash out against what today we still know as "pharisaism." Pharisaism is becoming so preoccupied with external, legal correctness to the point of neglecting the inner spirit of meaning and love. To be externally proper is good and desirable, but such external behavior must only be the outside measure of one's inner spirit. To have no or little inside love and to perform with accuracy all the outward motions of love—this is pharisaism.

Pharisaism has always plagued religion. It's our nature to start out with high ideals and end up with empty rules to promote those ideals. That is why Pascal said, "Everything starts out mystique and ends up politics." Even religion. If we don't watch it we wind up performing all of the correct actions and no longer do those actions tell accurately what's in our hearts. Not only that, but the actions begin to *substitute* for genuine virtue.

Are there Pharisees today? Listen once more to the description of Fathers Killgallon and Weber as they tell a story:

Charlie Williams approached the Pearly Gates with confidence. He should be well known in heaven, he figured. After all, hadn't he been a Catholic all his life? Not a convert, not one of those who come into the Church when half their life is over, but a bona fide "born" Catholic. Meat had never passed his lips on a Friday. Charlie was sure that the celestial books contained an impressive report on all the salmon and tuna fish he had consumed throughout a long and well-regulated life.

Charlie had no fears on the score of his Mass attendance record, either. He had never missed Mass on Sundays or holy days, except on a few occasions when he was sick in bed. And even on these occasions he had been careful to confess that he had missed Mass, "just to be sure." Charlie had been a faithful user of his Sunday envelopes, too. He was confident that his generosity to the Church Militant was duly recorded in the files of the Church Triumphant.

"It all sounds so familiar," said a dull, flat voice. Charlie whirled around. He had not been aware that he was thinking out loud. He had not been aware either that anyone else was about. Then he saw the owner of the voice—an old man with a long white beard. He was dressed in a silk, fur-trimmed robe which extended all the way to his sandaled feet. On his head he wore a white turban, and about his neck a gold chain. He looked for all the world like one of the figures in a Bible illustration, Charlie thought.

"Yes, you are right. You have heard of me," the bearded man said, as if he had read Charlie's thoughts. "I appeared in one of the parables of Jesus of Nazareth. I am the Pharisee who was immortalized by a visit I once made to the temple in Jerusalem."

Immediately into Charlie's mind leaped some words he had heard long ago. "Two men went up to the temple to pray, the one a Pharisee and the other a publican. The Pharisee stood and began to pray thus within himself: 'O God, I thank Thee that I am not like the rest of men, robbers, dishonest, adulterers, or even like this publican. I fast twice a week; I pay tithes of all that I possess.' But the publican, standing afar off, would not so much as lift up his eyes to heaven, but kept striking his breast, saying, 'O God, be merciful to me the sinner.'"

Charlie saw the point, and he did not like it. This Pharisee was an unbeliever. He had refused to accept Christ. Who was he to compare himself to Charlie, a life-long member of the one true Church of Jesus Christ?

Once again the Pharisee seemed to have read Charlie's thoughts. He shrugged. "Wait and see what the Lord has to say to you," he said. For the first time Charlie felt a slight stab of fear. "What did He say to you?" he asked, a little anxiously. "Don't you know?" the old Pharisee said. "He told me that I had all the satisfaction I deserved from the way I lived on earth. 'You have already received your reward,' the Lord said."

Charlie felt a stab again, but he quickly reassured himself. After all, the Pharisees were a pretty bad lot, quite different from himself. What could he have in common with a Pharisee? He was a Christian, and he had lived in the 20th century. What is more—he had been a "practical Catholic." He had not only gone to Mass every Sunday, he had been an usher at the eight o'clock Mass for years. Yes, he *had* been in the habit of ducking out for a smoke during the sermon, but after all that was no sin. The sermon was not a principal part of the Mass. "All you have to catch under pain of mortal sin is the Offertory, the Consecration and the Communion," he often said.

Yes, Charlie had been very careful to keep all the rules—all the rules which bound under sin. "Is it a sin?" he was always asking himself. This was his rule. His aim was to save his soul by keeping all the rules. For Charlie, this is what religion meant. His had been a religion of laws and obligations. God, he figured, kept pretty exact records, and he was determined that his score would be up to par.

In short, Charlie was a legalist, one whose religion was a matter of external observance, nothing more. In this Charlie was like the Pharisees.

But Charlie was right in one respect—the Pharisees as a sect disappeared long ago. Gone are the fur-trimmed robes, the turbans and the phylacteries. The Pharisees are gone, but pharisaism did not depart with them. The spirit of the Pharisees, the spirit against which Christ preached, is still very much with us. It shows up in many ways. Here are just a few of them.

A child in confession: "My mother said that I should go ahead and eat the meat on Friday, then I could go to confession on Saturday." The mother is not disturbed at the idea of sin, even serious sin. For her, mortal sin is simply a stain on the soul, which can be easily removed by the legal procedures of "going to confession."

A question about the Lenten fast: "Father, would it be all right if I skipped dessert at my main meal and had a piece of cake or pie as a snack later at night?" The questioner is not concerned with the spirit of the Lenten fast. She is not thinking of the love and spirit of sacrifice which alone makes self-denial meaningful to God. She is preoccupied solely with the law of fasting and with the extent to which it binds her.

One of the mourners at a wake: "I'd like to receive Communion at the funeral tomorrow, but I can't unless I go to confession first, because I had the flu last Sunday and had to miss Mass." The lady thinks that one can somehow become guilty of mortal sin even when one does nothing wrong. It is simply a legal penalty which one incurs for not fulfilling an obligation which one is not expected to fulfill under the circumstances.

Well you get the point so marvelously put by the authors. Unfortunately, Catholics in particular seem to have been caught up in this sort of thing. Somehow they have gotten the impression that if you do all of the outward things, this will satisfy God and He will have to give you grace. Not only that, but salvation is obtained by keeping the rules and the sooner you learn the ins and outs of religious rule-keeping, the better you'll make out in getting to heaven. The result of all this is to be careful to keep the minimum legal structures, period. To grow as a person, to run the risk of giving your all to God, to try to fill outward deeds with the content of love—this is not often tried.

The results of this morality is easy to see. Catholics have acquired a morality of the "minimum" and a morality of the rules. Like our friend Charlie Williams, we keep all the rules —but what about the weightier matters: justice and mercy and good faith? If we didn't eat meat on Good Friday about which there is an explicit Church law and yet treated our neighbor uncharitably about which there is the inner teaching of Jesus—can we say we are Christians? If we become terribly preoccupied with genuflecting the right way, folding the hands at the correct angle, bowing the head so many degrees that we don't have either the time or the mind left to really pray—can we say that we are Christians?

It is good to know the laws. It is good to keep the laws. It is better to fill those laws with love. It is better to know that in christian morality, as we saw in the last chapter, not every thing we ought to do is down on paper as it were; but that there is an inner spirit called the spirit of Jesus that should drive us on; that we *can* commit sin, not by breaking any specific rule but by failing in a general sense to love enough in concrete situations.

Christian morality is still summed up in the words of Jesus and Paul: "Love one another." How? By what standard? "As I have loved you." And Paul: "The love of Christ urges us on."

IV

The New Morality

1

That there should be a separate chapter entitled "The New Morality" will be significant for some. It will appear as a contrast to the preceding chapter on christian morality. Yet, strangely enough, the two, far from being at odds (at least in the eyes of the New Morality proponents), are quite complementary. In any case, no book purporting to give a general look at the new trends concerning sin and confession can ignore the subject.

Just what is it? The New Morality is not a well defined moral system but rather an outlook on life, an attitude, a general personal approach to the problems of human life. This morality claims to be "new" because the "old" morality was not only inadequate but static, unhuman and mechanical. At least this is what is said and, actually, there is enough of truth in this claim to bear investigation. We cannot here, within the confines of this book, delve into all of the isms, ethical solutions, situation ethics and moral directions that express various aspects of the New Morality. Rather for our purposes we shall examine some of the background that led to the emergence of the New Morality since, like most movements, it represents a reaction to what went before. Let us further narrow down our investigation not only to the youth who are its most active practitioners, but to the two fields where the New Morality has received the most publicity: the field of social responsibility and the field of sex.

The sophisticated youth of today are creatures of the world. Television has shown them every part of the globe, exposed them to every human need, every foreign culture and every exotic religion. As a result they have become acutely aware of world problems, national goals and personal aspirations. Yet they find themselves morally unprepared to respond to these problems. Why? Because, they point out, their christian education has taught them very little if anything about social responsibility. Catholics reveal that they have received very little in the way of social ethics and they are bitter about this. Rather they have been brought up on that legalistic morality of which we spoke before that stressed personal and not social responsibility. Eating meat on Fridays, missing Mass on Sundays and breaking the total and absolute rule of sexual abstinence in thought, word and deed before marriage constituted practically the sum total of their spiritual substance and moral guide. There was little sensitivity in acknowledging any discrepancy between going to Mass on Sunday and being filled with racial hatred the rest of the week; or contributing to the support of the church and paying an unjust wage. It wasn't always as blatant as this, of course, but the impression of the former moral teaching was that the Church took a great deal of care about one's personal purity (legal and sexual) but not too much concern about social responsibility. Hardly ever did the Church take a bold stand on the great social issues of the day. In fact, the suspicion was that the Church did not even recognize that there were social issues. The new generation of global minded youth have come to resent this and to look down on a moral system that has been so indifferent to world problems or social issues. It almost seemed that the Church was indifferent to people. Francis Carling, the youthful author (24) of the book *Move Over* (Sheed & Ward, 1969) whom we will quote again, speaks for the young Catholic intellectuals:

> . . . As the institutional church adjusted itself, it became difficult for it to criticize society or to demand conduct of its members which might conflict with social customs. In fact, the church seemed unwilling to make any rigid moral requirements of its members, except for sexual ethics. Not that the church was totally uncritical of society, but its attacks on materialism, pleasure-seeking and the "vices" of modern society were rarely aimed very clearly. Efforts to mobilize church membership on certain issues—such as the threats of Communism or pornography—always seemed to be campaigns that would be approved by the more conservative elements of society. It remained unthinkable that the American churches might, for example, condemn militarism or unfair business methods (p. 121).

There was more that rattled the young. Why all of the emphasis on a strictly personal morality? Was it not possible that groups and nations could be immoral? Why have Catholics as a group not pressed for a clearing up of the slums or (before Vatican II) taken part in ecumenism? Why have they felt no urgency in speaking up as a united church against the Nazi atrocities, the plight of the Jews or the infringement of civil rights? Catholics have not been noticeable in social action or community projects. Thus a whole area of morality seems to have been missing and the world cultured youth of today have become quite aware of this morality gap. The "old" morality was lacking in feeling for persons. The "old" moral education left much to be desired. Again, Carling recounts for us the shock of discovery of how inadequate this moral training had been. He observes:

> Students who went to the South, and even those who stayed home, were faced with racial hatred. This was a kind of sin they had not heard much about. The morality of grammar school, and even of high school, had been personal not social. It was based on individual responsibility for particular moral acts. There was very little notion that groups could be responsible for conditions which they could prevent. Sins of omission had been talked about, but the idea had never been applied to social responsibility. Moreover, there was a certain glibness in the morality we were taught. It was a standard quip of our own high school teachers that "You have to love your neighbor, but you don't have to like him." What this meant in effect was that as long as we "loved" black people— in some abstract but actually meaningless sense—we did not have to *like* having them around. That meant that it was perfectly moral to keep them from finding a place to live in our neighborhoods.

> The second revelation was that the Church was failing to install in her members a strong sense of this "social" morality. Catholic activists who were spending most of their time arguing with other Catholics about race hatred wondered what the point of all their theological training had been if it did not instill a vigorous moral sensibility. Perhaps it was not fair to blame the church for the political conservatism of her members, but the students could not help wondering whether there had been some misplacement of emphasis in their Christian education. Because of their identification with the outcast black community, these young people read the Gos-

pel teaching on the necessity of aiding the downtrodden with
a new insight: Christ said time and time again that his followers would be recognized by their love for their fellow
men. The whole complex structure of liturgy and doctrine
had failed to bring most Catholics to this simplest apprecia-
tion of Christianity. Many activists asked themselves, therefore, if being Christian had any necessary connection with
church structure (p. 98, 99).

Because of this "misplacement of emphasis in their Christian education" the young have sought a "new" morality, one
that is broader in scope. They have plunged heavily into
matters of social justice and civil rights. They have brought
to the forefront what the Church has neglected. They have
become disenchanted with "organized" religion and a one-
sided morality. The New Morality on social matters is very
personal, very involved and very active. In this area the New
Morality turns out to be one of literal Christianity. Older
people brought up on the "fish-mass-sex" moral summary
may shake their heads at all of the youthful activism and the
youth's ultra concern for war and peace and civil rights and
Vietnam; and the youth themselves may be criticized for
their ways and means, but in essence much of the New Morality in the field of society is a reaction against an old morality that excluded others and bred complacency over a few
legalisms. The youth are out to shake up the older generation out of that complacency and a fresh awareness of what
it is to be "my brother's keeper" is the tool they are using.

2

As the concern for persons rather than institutions of dog-
mas characterize the New Morality of social responsibility so
does this same concern form the ultimate basis for a reassess-

ment in the area of sexual morality. Here, too, the youth claim to find all sorts of contradictions and unrealistic legalisms. They have discovered the old sexual ethic of no sex whatever before marriage and everything afterward to be so mechanistic, so unrealistic and so impersonal that they cannot accept it. They may be willing to be moral and may even be open to come to the same conclusions, but they need a new basis to arrive at them.

Sexual morality has been mechanistic because it has been based, not on the persons involved, but on strict biology. Sexual relations would lead to disease, discovery and pregnancy, so they were forbidden. After marriage sexual relations could be devoid of all personal relationships as the wife was told that she must render the "debt" of intercourse under pain of mortal sin. Her role was reduced to a baby-producing machine and her personal feelings and growth did not matter. Before marriage anything whatsoever concerning sex was forbidden and always, of course, under penalty of mortal sin. This broad kind of morality was impossible to observe: the boys got a terrible sense of guilt for any ordinary bodily, sexual movements and the girls a sense of shame for thinking they might enjoy a caress. As the urgency of the sexual drive came to the fore with pubescence the strictures of religion were bound to look not only less attractive but less possible. Many wondered if such a narrow view of sex and such a suspicion of pleasure were truly realistic and truly christian. Again our young author speaks out:

> The sexual ethic was a simple rule-of-thumb: sex could not be enjoyed physically before marriage. Now it was not possible for us to date for any length of time without ending up kissing someone seriously, that is, in any other way than

we would on her doorstep, with her father looking on. Yet though this kind of behavior was demanded of us socially, we were taught that if we caught ourselves *liking* it we would damn our souls to hell forever . . . (p. 47).

The Church's strain over sexual morals, her emphasis on the subject led to a mental framework that we have not shaken yet: sex is morality and morality is sex. Equating purity with morality and impurity with immorality has become an almost exclusive correlative. If we are told that someone is doing something immoral we immediately think of sexual sins. As a matter of fact he may be hating his neighbor, exercising racial prejudice or cheating on his bill.

All of the rethinking about sex among the young received a great boost from the introduction of penicillin and the pill. No longer were the triple threats of infection, detection and conception meaningful. No longer was a sexual ethic based strictly on biology pertinent. New foundations had to be sought for being sexually moral. Indeed a new definition of sexual morality itself was needed. As the general line of the New Morality was extremely personal, so the personal approach to sex underlies the efforts at discovering a sexual ethic. The questions were to be, "Does this hurt a person?" "Does this exploit?" "Is this meaningful?" The answers and subsequent behavior to these questions may have, in some cases, proven shallow and self-deceptive but there's no mistaking their personal orientation. So, too, the sexual experimentation, sensitivity courses, communal living which shock and disgust the older generation are merely factors in the general search for a new personal basis of sexual morality. Since few people can maintain their equilibrium about sex it is not surprising that excesses have been prevalent and that some have gone into immorality without premise and promiscuity without restraint. Moral and psychological hurt have been apparent. Dr. Seymour Halleck in an article entitled "Sex and Mental Health on Campus" makes these observations:

> . . . If a girl accepts the new attitudes and wishes to have sexual relations with a boy on the basis of mutual affection and love, she must still define the strength of their commitment. Inevitably she must struggle with the questions of how close two people can be when not bound to one another by the responsibilities of a marital contract. Any relationship out of wedlock is plagued with certain ambiguities. . . . It is my belief that these ambiguities have been heightened by changes in attitudes towards sex. The stresses associated with choosing and sustaining sexual relationships before marriage have had an especially intense effect upon female students. For some students such stresses have been critical factors in precipitating severe emotional disorders. . . .

In any case, whatever the bypaths, the New Morality in sexual modes is not only the result of the pill but the result of the desire of the thinking young to put the basis of sex on a firmer basis than mere mechanical biology. Most are seeking for some personal basis. To say this is not to excuse the open sinfulness of some but to credit others with sincerity. It is to say, as Father Richard McCormick reminds us, that the young have rejected a mechanical legalistic approach to life in general and have sought to develop a more personal approach. They are seeking a New Morality.

3

Before we close this chapter, we must pause over a ramification of what we said in passing before regarding pleasure.

Since the tension of pleasure and sin causes much strain and anxiety on the average Catholic, it will pay us to make some observations. The first observation is the basic philosophical tenet that sin must be attractive in order for us to desire it. The whole psychology of temptation is built on this premise. The whole industry of advertising presupposes it. There must be some good to the sin, some appearance of delight, some usefulness else we would not seek it. Any sin that would be completely and totally evil in every respect would never be a temptation. Its total repulsiveness would prevent its being ever committed. Sin, therefore, must be attractive and must carry *some* good in it. Where does the sinfulness of sin come in? In simple terms, we might say that sin is sin because, *in the long run*, it destroys. Sin usually rewards with immediate goals but eventually harms. We apply this commonly with our children. *We* know that too much ice cream will bring immediate enjoyment but the eventual stomach ache. We caution our children against the harm of too-much. We know that all that glitters is not gold and that the shiney bike may be low in quality and we advise our offspring accordingly. We admit that stealing will bring present usefulness in paying one's bills, but hurt the moral fabric of society so that eventually much harm may be done to many. We admit that killing certain people will relieve an immediate problem but that to admit such a principle in civilization would destroy it.

So it goes. Sin usually has an immediate gain but brings ultimate harm. But what is our hangup? Our hangup is that we cannot emotionally (as a result of our training) keep the two elements separated. We keep wanting to apologize for the immediate joy in the sin and not just for hurting or wounding our friendship with the Father. This is the case of the boy who pets his girl friend and feels that he must be sorry for the sexual delight he received. On the contrary. His sorrow must go further to the implications for the personal uncharity he has done to the girl; he really cannot feel bad about the pleasure and he will have a difficult time trying to pull off this impossible feat. A married woman commits adultery and tries to include in her sorrow the joys of the affair. Her adulterous partner was, in fact, very kind to her; much more understanding and comforting than her alcoholic husband. She found some measure of happiness with this man. Can she be sorry for that? Rather her sorrow must be for the larger evil to marriage in general, to her husband in particular, to love in every direction. If she is a Catholic she will feel guilty that she enjoyed the enjoyable part of her sin and she will force herself into self deceit in order that she might experience regret and "true sorrow" over this "horrible" affair. It was horrible but hardly in *every* respect else she would never have begun it.

In Bruce Marshall's book *Father Malachy's Miracle* a few years ago, the priest is administering to an old sailor who was dying; he is trying to get him to make a good confession and repent for his sins. But the poor wretch couldn't really be sorry for his many affairs in each port. There was precious little comfort in his hard life and these brief affairs gave him the only moments of forgetfulness that he had. He couldn't in all honesty be sorry for what he did. Father Malachy, in the spirit of inspiration, then settles for this much: he asks the man if at least he can be sorry for not being sorry. This is good theology. The man was too unsophisticated to see the full ramifications of his immediate sins; he should at least be sorry for not seeing where the real sin was. Father Malachy wisely could not demand sorrow for the few momentary and fleeting joys this man ever experienced.

As Catholics we are very prone to guilt contortions especially in the area of sex. But to be truly human and truly christian we must experience sorrow for offending our Father, but not sorrow for what attracted us in the first place. We cannot and should not decry the legitimate pleasures God put into things. We can only regret that, in our own selfish way, we separated the pleasure from the larger responsibility. The child may indeed be sorry for his stomachache, but it is too unrealistic to ask him to denounce the ice cream eating pleasure that brought it on. So too the mature Christian. He must admit to what joy there was in his deed and then proceed to place his genuine sorrow where it really belongs: beyond the immediate attraction and temporary joys to the larger love-implications of his actions.

V

The Over-All Record

1

This will be a difficult chapter. It concerns a concept the theologians call the "fundamental option" and though disputed in all its ramifications by some, it is worth considering here. Let us begin with a simple and sympathetic example. A high school girl had a total of twelve science tests. In all of them she scored an "A," except one. In that test she received an "F," a failure. She is, of course, upset about that one failure but she figures that with all those other "A"s she ought to get a pretty good mark on her report card. Imagine her surprise and upsetment when she gets an "F" for the whole marking period! Her first cry will be, "But that's unfair!" She's right. Imagine one flunk out of twelve passing marks representing her total effort!

Take another school case. The principal calls in two boys who have done some mischief in school. To the one boy, Joe, he says, "Well, Joe, you've been in this school for seven years and for seven years we've had nothing but trouble with you. You've broken windows, bullied the kids and disturbed the class. Every teacher you've ever had has complained about you. We've given you enough chances. You are now expelled from school!" But to the other boy, Mike, who did the same misdemeanor with Joe, he says, "Well, Michael, I'm surprised at you. This is the first time I ever recall your being in this office. I can't imagine what made you do such a thing. Well, this is your first offense and I've talked it over with your teachers and we all feel that we'll give you another chance. I'll let you off with a warning this time. Now go back to class."

Notice the difference in treatment. Both boys committed the same misdemeanor, yet one is expelled and the other kept. Why? Or why did the girl get upset over the "F" on the report card? The answer to both questions is the same: because it is only right that a person should be judged, not on a single act, but on his over-all record. This explains the girl's chagrin and the principal's unequal punishment. We all make mistakes. None of us wants to be judged on these mistakes alone but rather on our general behavior. One error should not spoil our whole record. One mistake should not be final. In one of those delightful "Peanuts" cartoons, Lucy asks Snoopy to hold her balloon while she goes to lunch. Since she takes so long Snoopy, as is his custom, goes to sleep and when he yawns he releases the balloon. On the last panel of the cartoon you see Snoopy walking along the railroad tracks with his belongings wrapped around a stick saying, "Make one mistake and you pay for it the rest of your life!" Evidently, Lucy has expelled him for his one mistake.

Well, that's Lucy and that's cartoon stuff, but it's not life. Most people's tolerance level is high and most have a deeper concept of friendship that sustains many mistakes and many strains on it. Our friends may not be happy for our lapses but a real friendship endures and accepts much. It does not terminate over one bit of friction (unless it's so outrageous as not to be tolerated) but lasts. In other words, our friends tend to judge us in a larger pattern of service and love while leaving room for lapses within that pattern.

God does the same; and when such a concept is applied to Him the theologians call this the "fundamental option" or the "over-all record." They are saying that as our Friend, God is fair, just, kind, merciful and tolerant and has wide vision. One sin will not separate us from our friend forever (unless it is so outrageous as not to be tolerated). One sin will not put us in hell forever. Rather, God will judge us on our over-all record; He will look at our lifetime and *all* the things we've done. His judgment for our eternity will be based on our general pattern of preference for and service to Him in the course of our stay on earth, even though within this pattern there are individual lapses.

Thus the terms "fundamental option" or "over-all record" refer to the basic over-all direction of a person's moral life, his fundamental choice towards or away from God. The "over-all record" idea refers to the recognizable love-of-God pattern in a person's life resulting from a repeated series of decisions and actions. It is the general "tone" of the state of one's love of God. This "over-all record" forms a basic background against which individual actions and sins are to be seen; it is the general context in which isolated sins are to be measured as bearing on our final destiny.

Again, the "over-all record" is a term describing a person's moral pattern and underlining the fact that individual acts must be judged in this general context much the same way that the principal judged the boys' misdemeanors within their seven-year context. Or, to use other examples: one pulled thread (regretful as this might be) does not destroy the over-all cloth design. One slight angle flaws but does not nullify the general shape of a circle. One lie does not negate an entire pattern of truthfulness. So, too, one grave sin does not cancel a whole life-direction towards God.

The not infrequent question we get from adults or high school kids on retreats about the case of the ninety-nine year old good and faithful man who commits one serious sin on his hundredth birthday and then dies and so goes to hell is both invalid and unchristian. Worse, it is blasphemy. It makes of God, not the Father He declared himself to be, but an insensible and insufferable Monster waiting to catch His creature in an error and destroy him. The comment "one serious sin puts you in hell!" is theologically false. *God does not isolate man's actions as a basis for final reward or punishment*, but rather, as do human beings, He judges man in the sum total of his over-all record. Louis Monden, in his excellent work, *Sin, Liberty and Law*, expresses it well when he says:

Until the quite recent past the case of the person *damned for one mortal sin* was a favorite theme for retreat masters. Transposed into the foregoing terminology, the question is: Is it possible that in the first single action through which a person turns away from God in a fundamental way, thus committing a "mortal sin," his basic option might be so radically and so totally expressed that this choice would decide the whole direction of his existence, becoming for him concretely a "sin unto death" within which his free will would forever assume its position? The possibility of such an action could be discussed indefinitely. In practice, however, the probability is so slight that one need hardly take it into account. The treatment of this theme in the pulpit is a good example of the deformation of the truths of the faith which takes place when discussion is allowed to degenerate into a mere game of concepts without any contact with reality. With the best of intentions, hell, instead of being presented as the freely accepted, everlasting situation of the refusal of God, is mythologized into some kind of surprise roundup by the divine police of delinquents caught in the act—in their first robbery, for instance. Mortal sin is often materially conceived simply as doing something which is forbidden, with no account taken of circumstances or lack of experience which might make a really free choice impossible; instead of a moment within a development, it then becomes an autonomous event which automatically brings about its sanction, and which can only be undone by the almost equally isolated action (the counter-move) of a confession.

2

Having seen the meaning of the "over-all record" concept, we are now in a position to pick up a point we mentioned in the third chapter: that of mortal sin. You recall that we spoke of venial sin as hurting or wounding the friendship between ourselves and God in the sense of "annoyance" and "aggravation." We then spoke of grave sin as a serious hurt, a more severe blow that, while it pushes God out of our lives and demands confession for us, still leaves room for reconciliation, for recementing the friendship. Diplomatic channels are still open (v.g. confession, sincere declaration of sorrow, etc.). But with mortal sin, it is different. In order to understand the difference, let us look again in more detail at grave sin, reexplain it and then investigate "mortal" sin.

Grave sin is a serious matter. Something important has been done to the friendship but of itself alone, it does not send a person to eternal hell. Why? Because the deed is not strong enough and deep enough of itself *to pull a whole life pattern out of shape.* Grave sin is comparable to a severe quarrel between a husband and wife. As outrageous as this quarrel might be, there is no thought and no expression of divorce even mentioned. In spite of everything, they still remain together in the same house. So with God. As serious as grave sin might be, the relationship between God and the sinner, like the married couples', is still intact. It has not been completely broken.

For the average good person grave sin is the unrhythmed and freely done sin that was committed without undue influence. It is an isolated act with full consent and full knowledge; it demands confession. Isolated as it is, however, it is not a determining factor, by itself, for eternal damnation. That final punishment is the result of a general pattern, not a single act.

Without trying to add to the difficulty, I would digress here a moment to mention one more distinction as regards grave sin. I said that grave sin is the unrhythmed and freely done sin committed without undue influence. Those words were chosen purposely since there does exist an opposite condition. There is such a thing as a rhythmed, habit-pressured act pushing up through one's over-all love pattern. And this is *not* grave sin and maybe no sin at all. This is the act which is not a grave sin, not because it is not serious, but because in the person's psychological make-up, it is so strong as to normally overcome free consent (one of the essential conditions for sin—see chapter III). We can spot cases like this by simply noticing that, on the one hand, the person's over-all context of the love of God is very pervasive and, on the other hand, the force of the habit is strong. In other words, a person's over-all living is quite moral and christian, but he or she has a recurrent moral problem which distresses him and which he works hard to overcome. In spite of this, the force of habit is so strong as to overcome his resolutions. In cases like these we would have objectively grave wrong-doing but not necessarily grave sin because of the lack of freedom in the person. This is what the theologians have always called the force of passion lessening the freedom of responsibility. Examples might be drinking, masturbation, temper, etc. Such acts for the faithful Christian are not generally grave sins (although they can be on occasion) and do not need confession as such since concerning such wrong-doing full knowledge or full consent might be missing. As I've said, the over-all pattern of a well-lived life is a proof that passion, not deliberation, is at work here. In a word no one can have a strong, over-all love of God and still be breaking in a profound way his relationship with the Father several times a week! Sometimes it's not always easy to determine the distinction between actual grave and responsible sin and mere non-responsible passioned wrong-doing; but the distinction does exist.

Anyway, we come to what is properly called mortal sin. The word itself means "deadly" and is the key to its definition. This is a serious sin so severe and so strong as to truly "kill" the over-all pattern of the God-man relationship. It's like someone doing something so profound, so definitively treacherous and final to his friend that the friendship could not possibly endure. Or else, mortal sin is a serious action which is one more of many, many serious actions thus forming a definite negative pattern of living. Mortal sin is like the actual divorce of husband and wife. It's not just the severe quarrel which left them hurt and injured (grave sin) but it is the separation of complete divorce. Something has truly died: the friendship between God and man. Mortal or "deadly" are really the only accurate terms to be used of this condition. This is real mortal sin—the act or persistent series of serious acts that weave a pattern of unlove and selfishness that ultimately exclude God. It should be obvious that mortal sin in this sense is relatively rare in the life of a good Christian. People, of course, will continue to use the words loosely, saying mortal sin when they should mean grave sin. Perhaps it's all right to do so. But to know these distinctions is valuable and to keep in mind the nature and the framework of your relationship with your friend is worthwhile.

Before we give a further explanatory quote, however, let us pause to admit something to ourselves: uncomfortableness with these concepts. These distinctions I have given here might raise certain suspicions that the whole notion of sin is being watered down. But such a reaction is rooted in our childish concept of Christianity that sees things in the black and white terms of reward and punishment. Such a reaction is rooted in that mentality (of which we spoke before) that religion is a game we play with God to see if we can outwit Him by keeping enough of the rules to make it safely into heaven in spite of His efforts to keep us out. In such a game mathematics become important as we try to "increase in merit," gain "more grace" and be very very careful about whether what we're doing is mortal or venial sin and walking the narrow line between them. But if we see Christianity as the Father who loves, as the God-in-Christ who taught us to choose, not between the bad and the good but between the good and the better—then our approach here is valid. To talk of sin in terms of friendship broken or kept, to see God's judgment of us as a total-situation thing, to realize the dif-

ference between what is "grave" and what is truly "mortal"—
these are the beginnings of spiritual maturity.

But to our quotation, this from Fr. F. J. Heggen:

> We use the term *serious* sin, and do not speak of mortal sin,
> precisely because here it is still a question of decisions which
> are taken in an instant, on an impulse. We seriously object
> to the suggestion that life-deciding mortal sin might be
> located in one detached deed, seen atomistically, on its own.
> The nature peculiar to human existence is precisely such that
> we can never determine ourselves in one detached deed.
> Thus also in moral judgment the emphasis needs to be laid
> upon a man's design in life, the design in life which causes
> me to become myself in wishing to be with the other person,
> or which enslaves me to freely chosen self-alienation in
> isolation. Mortal sin is always the result of something, it
> presupposes a growth and development. Hereby we do not
> wish to deny that there are moments in which we experience
> ourselves as being placed before choice. However, when
> within a fundamentally virtuous plan of life the choice turns
> out to be a negative one we then speak of serious sin and of
> nothing more than that. We only wish to call *mortal sin* that
> which really separates man from love. For as long as we
> continue to use this term equally for "momentary," "loose"
> deeds we shall continue to further a development of con-
> science which cannot be called healthy. Then we shall also
> continue to hear the remark: "It's a bit hard that you get
> punished for eternity if after a good life you 'happen' to fall
> into mortal sin and die in that state."
>
> Certainly, within a fundamentally good direction someone
> can take on the attitude of a serious sinner. He can clearly
> go against his conscience, forget his place in the personal
> community. Then he will drag another into his particular
> world in order to subject him to it. In this case love does
> not seek its way with zeal, but is eliminated by selfish desire.

Nevertheless, the great difference from the fundamentally wrong attitude to life is that the possibility described above is a passing situation, a "detached" deed. It is kicking over the traces, not actually being oneself. For this reason the person will want to "make good" his offense: he is "not really like that" and therefore returns to himself. Not returning, not retracing one's steps, not fighting to do so, after the fascination of the moment and the confusion of the situation, can precisely be a sign that it was not a question of kicking over the traces, but the expression, the birth, or confirmation, of a negative attitude.

In sin man expresses himself as being against his neighbor, thus against God, with whom he is called to be in community. How does sin take place in this relation? Take marriage, for example.

Love for each other naturally does not exclude our often causing each other pain, being inconsiderate, taking the justified desires of the other too little into account, not living on the level of Christ's love. These imperfections and this falling short form the venial sins.

It is possible that in a normal, healthy marriage a deep insult to one partner may occur, a deed which is in fierce opposition to love and through which the husband or wife at this particular moment is clearly given second place. Must it now be accepted that a deep relationship between two people who try to be really good to one another is *immediately* shattered by a deed which goes against it? It sometimes seems so, but then looking more closely the deed which breaks the bond of union is seen to be the expression of an attitude and shows the insulted partner clearly that he or she had actually been deceived for quite some time. Even if the insulting deed were to be adultery, it does not immediately break up the marriage. If the other partner sees—and this is often extremely difficult—that it really was a foolish whim on the part of the other, but no more than that, then not only is forgiveness made possible but, in spite of great disappointment, the community of love is preserved in its essence from *both* sides. With neither of them is there a moment of breaking, of real separation. People grow towards one another: they also grow apart.

By speaking in this way we do not wish to minimize sin. We believe that man chooses good and chooses evil. But this choice of life only apparently takes place at clearly defined moments. A choice of life becomes continually transformed. Particular events have their own very great significance in the realization of this choice. Mortal sin, which really and definitively separates man from God's love—unless a miracle of grace take place—does not suddenly fall out of the sky. It is made possible through laxity, through being satisfied with the minimum [over a period of time].

As we said at the opening of this chapter, these concepts are not easy. The entire chapter bears rereading. But underneath all the technical distinctions try to see what we might call the very "human" nature of our relationship with the Father. Each point in this book, each chapter tries in its own way to reshape the reader's attitude that he is dealing, not with some force or power, but with love, with a living person who is all love, whose justice is always compatible with that love and whose vision sees among our poor and failing efforts the delicate pattern of an over-all response to His goodness.

VI

Conscience

1

Problems arise in arithmetic or in balancing the budget. You sit down, apply your mind to the problem and arrive at an answer. Or you want to buy a bracelet or a car. You figure available money, future payments, etc., and make a purchase judgment. You want to rearrange your room. Instead of moving all that furniture around you just stand there and in your mind's eye you picture new arrangements in your head, make your decision and then start moving. In all of these instances, you are using your mind and making practical judgments. When you use this same mind, this same process of judgment and apply such to matters concerning right or wrong, this is called conscience.

Conscience is figuring out things in the moral area and making decisions accordingly. We stress this mind, judgment-making process because conscience may conjure up all sorts of mysterious holdovers for the adult from sudden inspiration to that little small voice in the back of your head. But no, conscience is you using your mind on your problems;

it's just that the problems of decisions concern matters moral; it is the awareness of right and wrong doing.

It is evident that since conscience is mind-awareness on moral matters that this intellectual process is formed early and must grow constantly. True, each person is born with certain insightful instincts, certain intellectual potentials, but these must be developed and these can be subject to error and misinformation. What are the influences on the average person's mind-conscience? Well, for one thing we must give due credit to a kind of instinct about certain things being right or wrong. In the course of man's long history there are certain inherited mental postures that makes us "feel" that, say, taking another man's property is wrong. There is something inside man's consciousness that moves him to think certain things are right and others not right.

But beyond this there are many outside factors that have helped us and indeed shaped our consciences. The first and most important influence is that, of course, of our parents. We'll mention practical applications of this strong influence a little later in this chapter. Here we just wish to give statement of how truly forceful is parental molding of the young mind-conscience. Not that parents always sit down with their children and explicitly say, "Now, look, this is right and this is wrong." They do this to some extent, but by far the average child learns about right and wrong from what his parents *do* and from the existential realities of their value system. Parents' tone of voice, their priorities in daily living, their vocabulary, facial expression all of the myriad nuances of showing approval or disapproval are potent factors in determining the child's conscience, in determining how he will think, judge and feel about things in the future. If parents are very honest people, for example, honesty will be absorbed by spiritual osmosis by the child. If they swear a lot children will pick up both the words and the attitude behind that. If they go to church on Sundays, the children will grow up with that pre-fixed in their minds as a value and the basis for a moral judgment. And so it goes. Parents perhaps have the most influence on the formation of one's conscience. But there are others.

The community for one. By the community we mean all the other people in one's neighborhood, town and country. The way the people in the neighborhood act and live, for example, will to some extent be absorbed as a judgment basis by children. If the community, for example, will not allow Negroes in town, the child will likely grow up prejudiced (pre-judging). If the town dislikes Jews or Poles the child will grow up narrow and isolated. The community is there adding or subtracting its witness to right and wrong in many countless ways and thus forming judgment values for the young.

Then there's the Church. There's the Church in its theoretical doctrine, the Church as an institution, the Church as everyday people who are church-goers. There's the historical Church with its two thousand years' tradition. All in all the Church has much to say actively or passively and it influences people in their understanding of right and wrong. Perhaps more so since the Church poses as the custodian of public and private morals. Of course, the Church in many of its ramifications may historically not listen to the Holy Spirit or else not make the message loud and clear and so fail to make present the teachings of Christ. The Church, alas, can be guilty of prejudice or unkindness or racism or quarrelling or division and thus ever in need of renewal. This was admitted in the degree on ecumenism for example,

But in subsequent centuries Communities became separated from full communion with the Catholic Church—developments for which, at times, men of both sides were to blame.

But we must remember that the Church *is* Christ in the world and has an authentic voice and so is important in the forming of consciences. As mother and teacher from God the Church cannot, should not be ignored.

So these are some of the many influences in the formation of conscience: instinct, parents, the community and the Church. But this is only the formation. Since conscience is an intellectual faculty it must constantly be upgraded and refined; it must be educated. This takes study and work but this must be undertaken so that we may truly grow as human beings. We must constantly try to learn in a more sophisticated way what Jesus wants of us and how we can build up our mutual friendship. We must, as we have seen before, be students of love and love must be our ultimate guide in moral decisions. We must ask ourselves Christ-like questions: "Is what I am doing really an act of love for another? Does this build up the community? Would Jesus do what I am doing?" These are questions of conscience a Christian must ask.

Everyone must follow his conscience in order to be sincere. This was brought out by Robert Bolt in his play *A Man for All Seasons* when with characteristic insight and humor he has this dialogue between Norfolk and St. Thomas More:

NORFOLK: Oh, confound all this. . . . I'm not a scholar, as Master Cromwell never tires of pointing out, and frankly I don't know whether the marriage was lawful or not. But, damn it, Thomas, look at these names. . . . You know these men! Can't you do what I did and come with us, for fellowship?

MORE: And when we stand before God, and you are sent to Paradise for doing according to your conscience, and I am damned for not doing according to mine, will you come with me, for fellowship?

Yet we must be cautious here. We hear a lot about following one's conscience these days whether it be on birth control or conscientious objection or what have you. This is true, but we must be extremely careful to note that we have the obligation to follow an *informed* conscience, a conscience that you have taken the trouble to educate. Some people in quoting the dictum that one is bound to follow one's conscience give the impression that anyone can therefore act on whim. "If it's all right for me, if *I* think it's all right, then it can't be wrong!" Nothing could be further from the truth. No one can say that and let it go at that. Nobody by himself can just make up his own mind because the simple truth is that nobody is that smart and nobody knows everything. Following one's conscience means following one's informed and educated conscience. There must be consultation in important matters. Father Gerald Slyoan in his little book, *How Do I Know I'm Doing Right*, puts it this way:

I know I'm doing right if I try to be pure in intention in all I do—what Jesus called being "single-minded" or "utterly sincere" (see Matthew 5:8).

I know I'm doing right if I consult the teaching of Jesus Christ, Lord of the Church, in His own words in the New Testament, and Moses and the prophets whom He relied on, and Paul and those other Apostles who taught in His name.

I know I'm doing right when I consciously make my love for God through my concern for men (*this* man, *this* woman) the measuring-stick for every choice I make.

I know I'm doing right when I consult the whole Church to help me resolve my conscience: its bishop-teachers, its theologians and religious thinkers, its holy and learned men of my own acquaintance. In all I do I mean to seek the counsel of the brotherhood of believers—and not theirs alone but that of any men of good will.

I know I'm doing right when I remain faithful to my conscience, which I have done everything in my power to inform.

We might be more specific and say that the Christian in particular must consult four people. First, he must consult the Holy Spirit. He must pray and the more earnestly in proportion to the seriousness of the issue; he must ask for guidance and light. He must be humble and sincere in his seeking and only prayer will help him achieve these conditions. Secondly, he must ask the community. Not that the community is always right, but he would be foolish to ignore what older people have said and done, to ignore the consensus of the people. Thirdly, he must consult the prudent. Just as in legal matters he would ask a lawyer and not the doctor, so too he must ask the wise and the prudent. Especially if they have competence in this or that field. Fourthly, he must consult the Church. Not only the Church past but the Church present, the magisterium and the consensus of the faithful. He must seek advice of this Holy Mother. Then he decides. Then his mind-at-work on moral matters is a sincere and informed conscience and he will never be wrong in God's eyes if he follows out what he decides.

2

As we mentioned before, parents have a tremendous influence on the formation of their children's consciences. In this part we would like to explore this matter further. Children do inherit a whole life's posture: ways of thinking, speaking, emoting feeling, reacting and judging. Thus they inherit conscience also since conscience is the way a person feels and judges things to be right or wrong.

In the area of morality the child is born with no set of rules imprinted on his mind. He must learn them. And he learns them not from being told but from observing and absorbing the attitudes and values and moral system of his parents. In the field of religion we may put it this way. The ultimate faith of the child is derived from his parents and those around him. Children become moral through moral parents. Children learn to love God from the love of their parents. Children learn forgiveness from the forgiveness of their parents.

Many times parents give their child moral schizophrenia by acting on whim rather than consistent principle. For example, when company is there and junior throws his bread and jelly around, all laugh and remark how "cute." The next day when he does the same thing, he gets spanked! The parents are certainly confusing the child. Why is something wrong one day and all right another? Parents who stay home from Mass on Sunday but see to it that the children go: what is this but moral confusion? Either going to church is good or bad. If it is good why do not mommy and daddy go; if it is bad why is the child being "punished" and made to go?

There are other examples. All parents by word say to their children that stealing and cheating are wrong; yet Suzy hears daddy bragging at the dinner table how he cheated on his income tax or "fixed" a ticket. Lying is not nice yet Betty hears mommy on the phone giving out with some fantastic stuff. There's not a parent who does not want chaste and pure children; yet what is Billy to think when daddy brings home *Playboy* and drools over it and leaves it in the rack for Billy to see? All this is a way of putting the cliché that parents' actions speak louder than their words.

But there are even more basic areas to observe in the formation of the consciences of children. One is parental attitude towards God himself. Do they portray God as a monster or a real Father? "God will punish you!" spoken to a six year old is sheer nonsense. "Ah, ha, that's a mortal sin (he's scratching his behind) and you'll go to hell for that!" A four year old in hell? Why, they wouldn't keep him there. He'd upset the whole place! "God won't love you if you do that" is untrue and irreligious. God will love your child no matter how bad he is. He may not "love" the bad behavior, but He always loves His children. In this connection Father Trese's advice to parents in his wonderful little book *Parent and Child* is apt:

> Like all powerful tools, love must be used with caution. It must never, under any circumstances, be used as a weapon or used as a bribe or threat. A child never should be threatened with the loss of his parents' love if he misbehaves, or promised love if he does behave. The child should feel that, in good report and bad report, he can always safely count on his parents' love. They do not love him for the goodness that is in him; they love *him*, period, and still love him even at his worst. If a child does not have this feeling, then he is insecure now and will be an insecure adult (p. 70).

How much more do these words refer to parents' use of God as a threat or rewarder. How many adults today feel uneasy with God because He was presented as anything but a loving Father when they were children? And isn't it strange that parents who would use God as a threat or super policeman never give God minimal credit for what goes right? They never say things like this, "Oh, wasn't that a wonderful party. How good God is!" Or, "Look at those colors on the trees. Only God could make things so pretty!" "Yes, our house is nice, Karen, and we're so thankful to God for what He has given us." Parents should present God as a loving Father.

As we shall see in a later chapter children cannot commit sins. They can do many and quite trying misdemeanors and in the long years of discipline they must learn control. But this control, the whole secret of discipline, must be intimately connected with love. Again, to quote Father Trese:

> The secret of training a child to bear with frustration lies in the love for the child which the parent brings to the task. "Mother loves you too much to let you cut yourself on that glass ashtray; here's a pretty box to play with instead." Or, "Daddy loves you too much to let you lose your sleep. You must be off to bed now so that you can grow big and strong." No matter how unwilling the child may be to give up his own wants, the pain of frustration becomes more bearable if he can sense the love and interest which lie behind parental directives. The love he receives is a compensation for the pleasure he surrenders (p. 60).

Parents do not always use this positive approach with God in their children's lives. It is easier to exclaim that God will punish the nine year old for lying than to tell the child that God loves him so much that He doesn't want him to lie and so grow up and not be liked or trusted. It is easier to threaten hell than to explain to the child that God loves him *and* Johnny and he shouldn't have taken Johnny's toy.

Again, love must be stressed in the formation of conscience. We do or don't do certain things because they are either loving or unloving acts. All faults are reducible to not loving enough. The lying or stealing were not just that: they were a failure to "love one another as I have loved you."

The most essential place to learn this love is to observe and experience it in the home between the parents themselves. But many children never witness moments of genuine affection between mommy and daddy! They should hear and see explicitly that their parents love each other. True, they will witness the sharp words and the arguments and their little world will be threatened; but to witness the embrace, the kiss, the hug, the caress—this tells them that all is well and that love and love alone can make human relationship survive—and the God relationship as well.

There are two other comments on the formation of the consciences of children. One is warning, stated elsewhere in this book, of making a legalist out of the child. Legalism we repeat once more takes the form of getting excited about the wrong things or getting preoccupied exclusively about matters of the law. We can get terribly upset over women's wearing hats at church or not, but live quite comfortably with the most glaring racism and prejudice. We can be very precise about getting to Mass every single Sunday but fight and argue and encourage the most fearful uncharity all during the week. We can even be faithful and go to confession and tell God we're sorry for having offended Him and never once say to our spouse, "I'm sorry I said that. I really do love you." This sort of thing can be our heritage to our children unless our conscience sensitivity is increased and upgraded. Moreover parents do transfer legalism by stressing always the letter of the law but never its inner meaning. Merely to state that eating meat on Ash Wednesday is a sin leaves the whole story untold. Why? What connection does this have with love? Only to warn that it's not yet the Gospel or Offertory so we didn't commit sin by coming late to Mass teaches the child to "cut corners" with God and puts the emphasis on quantity and not on quality. If you love God and want to worship Him you'll try to be on time. If you're late it's not because you're worried about sin, but you feel bad that you had less of your time to be with the community for His public worship; like feeling bad at being late at Grandma's birthday party. There's no thought of sin here, only love. Therefore, parents should not plague the child with rules and regulations about church or religion and leave unmentioned the inner spirit. They should never give the child the impression that *not* doing certain things fulfills the law of Christ. The "love of Christ urges us on" cries St. Paul. That's the rule of thumb in teaching children religion.

The final comment is to respect the child's conscience. As he gets older, especially around 13 or 14 where real conscience is beginning to manifest itself, he requires more freedom to make up his own mind. In adolescence he will go through the criticizing stage where he begins to examine the things taught to him; he will struggle with their validity and eventually will adopt his own code. He must be encouraged to make some of his own decisions and judgments. Haim Ginott in his book *Between Parent and Child* puts it this way:

> A good parent, like a good teacher, is one who makes himself increasingly *dispensable* to children. He finds satisfaction in relationships that lead children to make their own choices and to use their own powers. In conversations with children, we can consciously use phrases that indicate our belief in

their capacity to make wise decisions for themselves. Thus, when our inner response to a child's request is "yes" we can express it in statements designed to foster the child's independence. Here are a few ways of saying yes:

"If you want to."
"If that is really what you like."
"You decide about that."
"It is really up to you."
"It is entirely your choice."
"Whatever you decide is fine with me."

Our "yes" may be gratifying to the child, but the other statements give him the additional satisfaction of making his own decisions, and of enjoying our faith in him (p. 89, 90).

In summary, let us mention once more that conscience is practical moral judgment, an awareness (which includes emotional overtones as well) of right and wrong doing. To be truly human is to make of one's conscience an ever more perceptive and expansive faculty. To be truly christian is to expand that conscience in accordance of Jesus' teaching on love. Those who are adults have a large responsibility in the formation of the child's conscience. What they do, and the love-ethic they show and the interior intention that they teach—all should coalesce into putting into the child that love which persistently urges him "to be perfect as the heavenly Father is perfect."

VII

Signs and Faith

1

"If your sins be as red as scarlet," the Father has said, "I will make them as white as snow" (Isaiah). And why should He do this? Because "I have loved you with an everlasting love" (Jeremiah). Yes, God is always willing to extend forgiveness. In fact, He initiated forgiveness by sending His only Son into the world to be our apology for sin since we could not accomplish this alone. It only remains for us, through baptism, faith and repentance, to take Christ's apology to ourselves and offer it to the Father. Jesus, on His part, makes this apology available to us. That is why His very name means "Savior" and those old signs we used to see outside of little chapels or storefront churches are true: "Jesus Saves." Saving indeed was His mission according to His own words:

> This is what the Son of Man has come for, to search out and to save what has been lost (Luke 19.10).

> I have come that they may have life and have it more abundantly (Jn 10:10).

I have come to call sinners to repentance (Luke 5:32).

The Son of Man did not come to have service done him; he came to serve others and to give his life as a ransom for the lives of many (Matt 20:28).

This is my Blood which shall be shed for you and for all men so that sins may be forgiven. . . .

His Apostles have added their testimony:

In the Son of God, in his Blood, we find redemption that sets us free from our sins (Col 1:14).

You were not redeemed with corruptible things such as gold or silver . . . but with the precious blood of Christ (1 Pet 1:19).

In this is love—not that we have loved God, but that he has loved us and sent his Son as a sacrifice for our sins (1 Jn 4:10).

If, therefore, we make ours the pleading of Jesus, we can find forgiveness for the Father always listens to His Son (Jn 11:41). By praying "through Christ our Lord" we can confidently approach the Father to experience this forgiveness.

This approach, however, has many variations. We can, for example, approach the Father in the search for forgiveness by sincere prayer. We can do acts of love expansively and specifically to cancel out our acts of unloving friendship. We do do acts of mortification. There are many ways that people can find forgiveness. The pagan, the devout Jew, the sincere Protestant—all have access to forgiveness through such approaches (although, even unknowingly, always through Christ). The Catholic, too, has these same avenues open to him but he has also a further belief about the forgiveness of sins. The Catholic believes that there is from Christ a special "signalling" or ratification that our sins are forgiven. He believes that Christ has left mankind a very particular form by which we can authenticate our sorrow and reconciliation. He believes that Jesus has left us a very special encounter with Him that officializes our renewal of friendship. This special encounter is called Confession or, better, the Sacrament of Reconciliation.

Now note that Catholics do not strictly need to go to confession to have their sins forgiven. As we said, the Catholic, like the devout non-Catholic, can find forgiveness through penance, love and charity. In fact, we are all familiar with the teaching about "perfect" contrition: that one can be forgiven outside of the sacrament of confession by sorrowing out of the highest motives of love for God. Why, then, confession? Because, as we said, confession is Jesus' way of officializing our forgiveness. It's His personal way of giving us a sign of the reality of our reconciliation. It is a more humanly secure way of feeling confident in our renewed friendship. It might be likened to the Governor of the state telling you over the phone that he's accepted your apology for campaigning against him in the last election: his conversation is sincere and all is well. But how much better, more secure, more "authentic" to receive an official letter on his stationery assuring you of his friendship and declaring his good will.

In the same way, although the Catholic can technically have his sins forgiven outside of confession, he opts for forgiveness in the sacrament because of the genuine and encountering authenticity he finds there. He finds it more secure and realistic to have Jesus through and before His whole Church ("on official stationery" as it were) reach out to openly and publicly proclaim reconciliation. But beyond this, (outside of an emergency or other most difficult circumstances), the Catholic must seek out Christ in the confessional situation to have his grave sins forgiven because he believes this is the will of Christ himself and the discipline of his church.

Why does the Catholic believe this to be Christ's will? Because he knows from history that his church has always had experiences of official repentance as varied as these may have been throughout the ages. He knows the experience and words of Christ Himself Who could forgive sins, since He was God, and who *did* forgive sins; for example the man in Luke 5:17 who had his sins forgiven and then his body healed to back up the reality of the inner forgiveness. He knows that Christ could pass on any of His powers to others, even mere men. He knows that Christ actually did do this. The Oxford (Protestant) New Testament records this scene in John 20:19 thus:

> Late that Sunday evening, when the disciples were together behind locked doors, for the fear of the Jews, Jesus came and stood among them. "Peace be with you!" he said, and then showed them his hands and his side. So when the disciples saw the Lord, they were filled with joy. Jesus repeated, "Peace be with you!" and then said, "As the Father sent me, so I send you." He then breathed on them saying, "Receive the Holy Spirit! If you forgive any man's sins, they stand forgiven; if you pronounce them unforgiven, unforgiven they remain."

2

It is essential to note that when Jesus did give to men the power to forgive sins He did so through outward signs. More accurately, when Jesus did decide to reach out to men through time and space through His Church He made this reaching, this touching, by means of signs. So vital is this concept of signs to the understanding of Christ's action on us that we must spend some time on seeing what precisely a sign is.

A sign is, quite simply, something on the outside that tells us about something on the inside. A sign is a symbol. It's a symbol that tries to get across all kinds of meanings, definitions and attitudes that are essentially spiritual and invisible. Everybody uses signs or symbols to be outward indicators of certain invisible postures and mystiques. Commercial industries specialize in outward signs that try to sell, not only their products, but the inner attitude that is supposed to go with them. Ford calls one of its cars "Mustang." The company is not trying to sell a machine that will get you from here to there, but a whole pattern of status. "Mustang" is supposed to evoke nuances of power, tang, snappiness and a little wildness tossed in for good measure. The customer is not only buying a car: he's buying a way of life; he's letting everyone know that, beneath his calm exterior, he too is something of a "Mustang." Can you imagine calling the same car "Sloth"? Nobody would buy the car no matter how good it was! The Space center called the first moon landing apparatus "Columbia" and "Eagle"—names symbolic of Jules Verne's moon rocket and our country's power and determination. Then there's CITGO, SPARKLE, GLEEM toothpaste, etc. All these are symbol names trying to tell the customer about supposedly inner qualities not visible to the eye.

Words are signs. These words here are just black lines on a white piece of paper. They are arranged in such a way that you recognize that they mean something invisible. They are outward signs of my invisible thoughts.

The children in school, when they know an answer (which is invisible), what do they do? They make an outward sign. They raise their hands. The hand-raising is the outward sign that the child possesses invisible knowledge. Knowledge is a spiritual commodity. It has no feel or smell or shape or size, etc. To declare such an invisible reality one must resort to outward, visible signs.

The best things in life are invisible. Justice, kindness, truth, love. Friendship. We've spoken of that. Look at how people spend most of their lives trying to express in outward form friendship and love. We have music, gifts, valentines, wedding rings, flowers and a million other things which try to get across the one invisible reality, "I love you!" Everybody uses signs. We are a "sign" people. We are signs ourselves. Our bodies, in fact, are the greatest signs we possess. We smile when invisibly happy, frown when angry, cry when hurt. We dance the body in joy and bow it low in worship. Our body is very expressive. It expresses us, the person. It is our personal sign of the inner "I."

We spent some time on this because the notion of sign is very important. The reason is that Jesus always accommodates himself to us and since we are sign people and deal with signs, so does He. He, in getting across to men, resorts to signs also. In fact, He invented seven outward signs in His special encounters with men. These signs are sacred and we call them sacraments since the word "sacred" is in that word. These seven sign-sacraments are visible signs that tell us about and cause invisible realities. Let's take one we're familiar with: baptism. What is invisible? Well, there's the baby's soul or spirit, the friendship-grace with God, original sin. What is visible? The baby itself, water (which we associate with washing or cleansing), and words. In this sacramental encounter Jesus is saying in effect, "Every time you see the baby being washed clean on the outside, this is a symbol that shows and causes the baby's soul to be clean on the inside. This outward sign of cleansing is an indication of My inner working of cleansing and adopting." The anointing with oil in Confirmation, the bread and wine in the Eucharist and the others are all outward sacred signs signifying and causing inner spiritual activity with Christ.

The sacrament of penance or reconciliation has its sign too. Before we see what this sign consists of, let us see what the invisible reality is that it is trying to express. Well, obviously, any outward sign of penance must try to express sorrow (which is a form of love). We're really sorry that we've damaged our friendship with God Who's been nothing but good to us and Who loves us so. Now, how do you indicate you're sorry since sorrow itself is invisible? There are many ways. Normally, people use the outward sign of speech: they say they're sorry. They apologize. On the other hand, maybe they'll indicate their sorrow by the way they look or a gift simply given.

It's the same in confession. Normally the outward sign of sorrow in the sacrament of reconciliation is *telling* your sins. You mention the kind of sin and the number of times and that usually indicates the sorrow of your heart. (As we'll see later in this chapter, we presume that the outward sign and inner sorrow match.) Again, telling one's sins is the normal outward sign of the inner reconciliation of the penitent and the Father, the normal expression of apology. But notice I use the term "normal." I use this term because there are other signs we might call "abnormal" that are just as good. For example, if telling one's sins is the normal outward sign of inner sorrow, what if you can't talk? Then you must resort to writing your sins or blinking your eyes or some other such signal. Sometimes there are times when such "abnormal" signs are more meaningful and intense.

Look at Mary Magdalene. She had sinned and she was sorry. She really wanted to tell Jesus that she was sorry but she got all choked up. The only thing she could do was to fall at His feet and cry. Her tears were a beautiful and sincere outward sign of her inner sorrow. She was forgiven because, as Jesus commented, "Much has been forgiven her because she has loved much." Mary Magdalene went to confession. She couldn't emotionally make the normal sign of telling her sins, but her tears spoke louder than her words and she was absolved.

In Luke 18:13 Jesus told us the story of the two men who went to confession as we would say today. The one man, the Pharisee, made a perfect confession exteriorly when he told his faults, "I fast, I give money to the church. I am not like this other sinful man here." The other man didn't say a word Jesus said. Rather he just knelt down in the back of the church and struck his breast with his fist and from the bottom of his heart muttered, "Oh God, be merciful to me, sinner that I am!" Jesus said that this man went away absolved rather than the other. Now notice, he did not tell his sins, the number or kind; just a cry from his heart to the Father.

Now I am not saying that it is not necessary to tell one's sins; I am just pointing out that the telling is *not the essence of confession*, but rather the inner sincerity is. I am saying that there are exceptions to the general rule of telling and that these exceptions are reasonable since, after all, forgiveness is given, not for the words we say, but for the sorrow they indicate. So true is this that we in fact can be in error about our sins; for example, telling some sins we really didn't commit or actually forgetting others we should mention. It makes no difference since the confessing itself is only a sign of something deeper: our genuine sorrow, our sincere desire to restore the friendship. Even the priest can misread the outward sign and still there will be no harm since again God forgives the inner reality, not the mere outward symbol. Louis Monden puts it this way:

> The priest in the confessional is one who, in God's name, utters God's releasing word over the sin. . . . What the penitent tells him is only a sign of what he tells God. The confession of sins is a sincere signifying . . . of his being a sinner before God. And the priest's judgment is only a sign of the merciful judgment of God. . . . Both penitent and priest may be wrong in their judgment about the confessed sins . . . if both are in good faith, this mistake does not matter at all, for God forgives not what has been confessed, but what has been signified by the confession.

That last sentence summarizes our point here. We are dealing with signs which are only signs. They are symbolizing something deeper: sorrow, friendship and love. The signs are important but we shouldn't get so preoccupied with them that we forget that they are only symbolic of something else. Moreover, there are times when the normal sign of telling one's sins can be discarded altogether and still there can be a true reconciliation. Beyond the examples of long ago such as Magdalene and the publican there are present day examples of soldiers going into battle: they may receive absolution without first telling their sins. People in hospitals where they might be overheard can have their sins forgiven without telling them as long as they are sorry in their hearts and give some indication that they are sorry. The unconscious can have their sins forgiven in the Sacrament of the Sick. All such instances point out the main point that in confession the important thing is not the telling of the sins but rather the inner love and sorrow in the heart. This concept also explains why a forgotten sin in confession is automatically forgiven. The sincerity of a person's heart covers all of his sins. Just because he really forgets to make a verbal outward sign doesn't mean that the inner reality of universal sorrow is not there.

Thus, the sacrament of reconciliation, like all of the sacraments, is a sign-encounter with Jesus. It is two people working through signs to reach the common ground of a restored friendship. We have seen that the telling of our sins is our normal sign we bring to the encounter. What sign does Christ bring? He brings the Church's words of absolution. These words are, "I absolve you from your sins in the name of the Father and of the Son and of the Holy Spirit." The words preceding these have been changed in recent years from Latin to English and even in content. This is because the Church desires that sign and action be more in harmony. Christ's sign, of course, signifies the Father's infinite mercy.

The sacrament of reconciliation, then, is two persons meeting to exchange signs. They exchange signs as indicators of the inner realities of forgiveness, sorrow, love and friendship. The sacrament of reconciliation is a real encounter between friends.

3

Before we leave the subject of sacramental signs, we must make one final point which is only a variation of what we have said previously. We must constantly renew the inner content of these signs. Or, to put the matter more succinctly, we must approach the sacramental sign of confession with faith. Let us turn once more to the Belgian spiritual writer, Louis Evely, for further insight to this question. In his justly famous book *That Man Is You* he describes the following scene:

Even when He lived on earth,
　He made no particular impression
　　on those who thought He was just another man.
One day, as a crowd milled around, jostling and elbowing Him,
　a woman drew near
　　　with faith in her heart and one thought in her mind:
　　　　"If only I can touch the tassel of His cloak,
　　　　　I'll be healed!"

　　　　She did—and was healed.

Then Jesus stopped.

"Who touched Me?" He asked.
Dull-witted as usual the Apostles answered,
　　"Master, how can You ask such a question
　　　when there are so many people
　　　　pressing about You on every side?"

But He ignored them and insisted,
　　"Someone touched Me.
　　　I can tell My healing power's been at work."

By this time, everybody realized something serious'd happened.
　They held their breath and backed away,
　　then blurted out:

　　　"I didn't do anything!"
　　　"Don't look at me!"
　　　"I didn't even come near Him."

And the poor woman,
    trembling and alone in the circle they'd cleared,
admitted, "The one who touched You—it was I."

Now, everybody'd touched Him,
    everybody'd hustled Him;
        still, nobody'd been cured or transformed.

Only one had touched Him with faith;
    and a profound sense of well-being coursed through her:
        she was cured.
                        (pp. 39, 40)

This moving and dramatic scene once more underscores a constant theme of this book: we must have faith, sincerity, inner intention. We spoke of pharisaism in another chapter. In the light of what we have just seen about the nature of signs we can describe pharisaism as signs without faith. In Catholic circles an over emphasis on the outward signs has led to a neglect on the inner meaning and disposition of the person. The result has been the emergence of a kind of "Catholic voodoo" as regards the sacraments. Just perform the signs in all of the minute correctness and automatically you will force God to give you grace. In the old catechisms people were taught (correctly) that the sacraments work *ex opere operato;* that is, automatically. They did not depend on the minister to be effective. In their own right they worked. True; but as Karl Rahner says, "The efficacy of the sacrament is measured and limited by the disposition of the penitent."

The sacraments in general and confession in particular "work" only if, like the woman in the Gospel story, we approach Jesus with faith. In the case of the sacrament of penance this faith takes the form of confidence in the mercy of

Jesus, belief in His saving power and genuine sorrow for the sins committed. Therefore (to quote Fr. Rahner again) "sins for which we are not really sorry are not remitted by the sacrament" (p. 197). The Church herself took note of this when in her decree on the sacred liturgy she said (italics mine):

> The purpose of the sacraments is to sanctify men, to build up the body of Christ, and finally, to give worship to God; because they are signs they also instruct. *They not only presuppose faith,* but by words and objects they also nourish, strengthen and express it; that is why they are called "sacraments of faith" (no. 59).

This sounds so obvious, but we have many years of the "magic" approach to confession to overcome. The once-a-year Easter duty confession, the socially-pressured wedding confessions, the forced children's confessions—all these are empty gestures without faith. We can all press in on Jesus, all crowd with our signs into His confessional box, but only those people who touch Him with faith shall be saved.

VIII

Sin and Community

1

On July 20, 1969, the first human being set his foot on another celestial body other than the earth. Undoubtedly this was the most spectacular event in the history of mankind. So awesome was this event, so fraught with meaning and adventure for the whole human race that millions of people around the globe stopped to watch this historic episode on television. Friend and foe, rich and poor—all forgot their personal cares and personal enmities in the interest of what was obviously significant for all men. Perhaps as no other occurrence, the landing of man on the moon pointed up the basic unity of the whole human race. The instant communication of the era was heightened as it welded all men to one fantastic event that would continue to affect humankind for ever after.

Because such feats as instant video communication and moon landings reach out to all it is easier for us today to appreciate the unity of humankind; easier, at any rate, than in a former era where we lived in isolation and most of the parts of our planet were only exotic names to us. Thus with our

easier sense of human solidarity we can better understand
the subject of this chapter: the revival of the relation of sin
to the community at large. I say "revival" because sin in relation to the whole community is not a new concept. It goes
back to the earliest pages of the Bible. However, with our
political isolation and naive nationalism we soon narrowed
sin to only a problem between God and self, a strictly private
affair that we would take care of in secret. Yet, sin like love,
is a community affair and this is because we, though unique
individuals, make up one living Church, one Christian community, one Mystical Body.

Long ago St. Paul gave us the most graphic description of
our unity as one Christ. He likened our close-knit union to
the parts of a human body. He said:

> For Christ is like a single body with its many limbs and
> organs which, as many as they are, together make up one
> body. For indeed we were all brought into one body by
> baptism, in the one spirit. . . .

Paul is saying that just as the human body has many cells so,
too, Christ in His mystic state on earth, has many cells: the
baptized people throughout the world. Individually we are
who we are but together we add up to something more: we
are Christ. St. Paul gets more emphatic: "If one organ suffers,
they all suffer together. If one flourishes they all rejoice together. Now you are Christ's body and each of you a limb or
organ of it. . . ." In other words, if my toe hurts, *I* am un-
comfortable. Me, the whole person. If my stomach is taking
in ice cream, I, the whole person, am enjoying it. This is because, although I am made up of many parts, there is just one
I, one ego, one person. So, too, with Christ. There are baptized butchers and bakers and candle-stick makers, and
baptized doctors and truck drivers, and students and priests—

and together, forming the parts of one living Christ in the world, they affect one another.

Actually, this concept was not entirely original with St. Paul. He was really copying Christ himself. Jesus' own example was that of a Vine and branches. He said:

> I am the Vine, you are the branches. He who dwells in me as I dwell in him bears much fruit for apart from me you can do nothing. . . .

Have you ever seen grafting? This is a means whereby a branch from one tree is cut in a pointed shape and stuck on the branch of another tree cut to receive it. Then where the branches are joined, they are taped together. Soon the life-giving sap from the mother tree begins to flow into the newly adopted branch and before long this new branch is living with the same life and becomes part of the tree. Jesus says that union with Him is like that. At baptism we are "grafted" onto Christ, the living vine. His divine friendship-life of grace begins to flow into us making us holy with His very own holiness. Now we are Christ. He is the vine and we the branches but together we form one tree.

But we must not stop here. We must proceed to the next logical step. If at the moment we are "grafted" into Christ by baptism we become united with Him, so too we necessarily become united with all the other baptized members. It's like putting a new spoke into a wheel. Not only does the new spoke set up a relationship with the hub, but, by that very fact, it sets up a new relationship with all the other spokes thus joined to the common hub. Or, to return to Jesus' own example, I cannot be joined to the trunk of a tree without automatically setting up a necessary relationship with all the other branches.

So, while I maintain my individuality, I move in constant relationships. What I do or fail to do will of necessity affect others. I can no longer pretend indifference any more than the first man on the moon could pretend that he was doing this for the United States only. My actions now vibrate all the others. And this includes my sins. As a member of the christian family my sins, however private, will affect the entire Mystical Body. If I sin I detract from the community's total growth potential. I walk away from my brothers in Christ. If my sin is grave enough I may even shame my community into expelling me. As a matter of fact, this was precisely the situation in the early christian community. Father Jerome Murphy-O'Connor in an article in *Theology Digest* entitled "Sin and Community in the New Testament" describes it this way:

> . . . It is clear that sin poses a community dimension. If one sins he not only offends God, but injures the community as well. The primitive Church knew this at least existentially as her practice indicates. The community felt obliged to protect its impeccability. While the responsibility devolved especially upon her leaders, all members were asked to avoid creating the occasions of sin (1 Cor 8:11-12; Heb 3:12), counsel and exhort (1 Thes 5:11, 14; Heb 3:13-14), pray for one another (Jn 5:16; 1 Jn 5:16-17), and practice fraternal charity. Since the Christian, moreover, is not saved as an individual but as a member of the body of Christ, the Church must expel the hardened sinner because his belonging is a lie.

Bernard Haring, in his book *Shalom*, says this:

> But every sin, besides striking out at Christ, likewise strikes out at the family of God. The one who says "No" to God

says it within the realm of the people of God, by disassociating himself, by distorting the harmony of the family of God.

Each individual member of the Church, realizing the wealth of grace which he has deprived the Church by sinning, should do penance, seeking the forgiveness of the whole Church for what he has done to her. To some extent every sin means persecuting Christ in the Church. By sinning a man not only loses his true self, the personal perfection expected of him, but he also hurts the Church.

It is clear now that we have this mystic unity with one another in Christ by virtue of our baptism. It is equally clear that we spiritually interact and that, in a sense, no sin can ever be wholly private because the community, the Church, has a stake in our moral progress or regress and if and when we sin we offend the entire People of God.

2

If sin separates us from our brothers, what about repenting? Shouldn't that also involve the community? Certainly. It should and, in the history of the Church, it has. Repentance and reconciliation are community affairs. This community wide involvement with the sinner was quite apparent in the early church and in the middle ages. At these times there were public confession in the sense of proclamation of one's sinfulness and public penance. For example, a Christian of the eleventh or twelfth century who had sinned notoriously was put out of the church on Ash Wednesday or excommunicated. This excommunication is a literal matter: being cast away from the communion table. After all, the Eucharistic table is *par excellence* the focal point of christian unity; notorious members surely would be out of place there.

Such an expulsion from the table of the Lord finds an easy counterpart in our own everyday experiences. A child is fooling around at the dinner table. Warnings go unheeded and finally the father gets so annoyed that he shouts, "All right, now. That's enough! You get away from the table if you can't conduct yourself like a gentleman!" And the child leaves. He's cut off from the family meal, a temporary semimember, deprived of full participation. The early Christians went through the same routine. "Ex-communication" was getting put away from communion, being reduced to a kind of semimembership and being deprived of full meal-time participation.

The expulsion from the Christian family table lasted all Lent. Finally, the bishop would come—he, the president of the local community—and he would go down the aisle of the church towards the locked doors, on the other side of which were the penitents. They would hear him coming and cry out. The bishop would ask what they wanted and they would proclaim that they were sorry for their sins and wanted dearly to get back to the table of the Lord and eat the same Eucharistic food as the rest of the people. The bishop would then order the doors to be opened and would lead the penitents into the sanctuary. There they would admit their faults, receive absolution and be allowed to share in the family meal once more. It is most meaningful and significant, of course, that this ceremony took place on Holy Thursday, the birthday of the institution of the family meal for Christians. In fact, the whole sacrament of penance is basically orientated to the Eucharist; it is geared to make us more "fraternalized" so that the celebration of the Eucharist itself will be more full and perfect. The theologian Bernard Cooke, in his book, *Christian Sacraments and Christian Personality*, writes:

There is no sacrament whose externals are more clearly social in nature than those of Penance. This sacrament involves an exercise of judgment by an authorized delegate of the Church community. The purpose of his judgment is to reinstate the individual into the community, to reconcile the Christian more deeply to the Church to which he has been more or less unfaithful. Penance achieves this reconciliation in order that the community as a whole may be prepared for fuller participation in the sacrifice of the Mass. Viewed in this perspective, the sacrament of Penance, like all the other sacraments is intrinsically ordered to the full expression of Christian life in the action of the Eucharist. Its purpose is to purify and prepare the community for a fuller and more integral expression of its dedication to Christ (p. 88).

After the reconciliation took place, the whole congregation sang and praised God. The point is how deeply the christian community felt itself involved in sin and repentance; how their consciousness of the social effects of sin led them to a social event of reconciliation. Notice, too, that we said they all sang and praised God together on Holy Thursday. Even this is significant and finds its origin in the teaching of Jesus who brought out sin's community aspects. For example, when He told His famous story on confession, the prodigal son, He had the father say at the end:

Quick, fetch a robe, my best one and put it on him; put a ring on his finger and shoes on his feet. Bring the fatted calf and kill it and let us have a feast to celebrate the day. For this son of mine was dead and has come back to life. He was lost and is found.

Note the community participation, the community rejoicing, the community celebration. In other stories Jesus emphasized the social aspect of sin and repentance. He said in His parable of the lost sheep:

> Rejoice with me. I have found my lost sheep. In the same way I tell you, there will be greater joy in heaven over one sinner who repents than over ninety nine righteous people who do not need to repent.

Here even the court of heaven celebrates over this one sinner. We ourselves reflect this union with heaven in our *Confiteor* where we confess not only to Almighty God, but to Blessed Mary ever-virgin, blessed Michael the archangel, blessed John the Baptist, the holy Apostles, Peter and Paul and all the saints. Such a litany affirms the reality of community interest and concern and participation in the repentance of sin. Vatican II in the *Constitution on the Church* carried the idea forward to the present time when it said:

> Those who approach the sacrament of penance obtain pardon from the mercy of God for offenses committed against Him. They are at the same time reconciled with the Church, which they have wounded by their sins, and which by charity, example, and prayer seeks their conversation (no. 11).

3

It is obvious to all that we have lost this community sense of sin and repentance in the last centuries. So-called private confession—even though the priest is actually there as community representative—has become so private that it has obliterated the rich heritage of community penitential concern of the past eras. And now, at least at the present time, with so many private confessions falling off and those long Saturday night lines down to a trickle, there is a need to revive the older forms and older emphases. Once more, Vatican II in her decree on the sacred liturgy recognized the need for change. "The rite and formulas for the sacrament of penance are to be revised so that they may more clearly express the nature and effect of the sacrament" (no. 72). As indicated before, some changes have been made and more will be made. The words of absolution are in English and the words themselves have been changed and will be altered in the future. But this is probably not enough. The liturgy surrounding penance itself must be expanded to include this social consciousness. To meet this need there is gaining rapidly the custom of communal confessions. Their logic and place is explained by Father Gross in his booklet of ten "Celebrations of Penance":

> Today in the Church there is need of enriching our present sacramental practice in the light of that former community or ecclesial dimension. This is the reason for the return of common celebrations of penance. They are a help to the sinner, for he prepares for his confession with others while praying and singing together. Those gathered around him bring their faith and hope to bear on his weakness, by their very presence showing their christian concern for him. Preparing for penance in common is a reminder, too, of the terrible social damage that is caused by sin. It enables the erring one to see that his wrong-doing is not a private affair between himself and God but that it always involves an offense against Christ present among men, Christ present in his neighbor. A celebration of penance is meant to be a sign, a sign however much more potent than it has been in recent church practice . . . (p. 6).

Communal confessions, then, are public celebrations of the sacrament of reconciliation. Basically, a communal confession is a bible vigil, that is, singing and readings surrounding the reception of the sacrament. Communal confession celebrations vary but most have certain constant elements. A typical service would take this order. The people gather and walk in procession into the church singing some penitential song together. Then there is a Scripture reading underlining some aspect of the mighty saving works of God. This may be from the Old or New Testaments. For example, readings from the Exodus or the story of the Prodigal Son or Mary Magdalene, etc., might be rendered. These readings are followed by a homily and by periods of silent prayer and then a hymn. After this there is a common recitation of the first part of the *Confiteor* and, in some places, a public examination of conscience read by the lector. Next there is provision for private confessions for those who must go or wish to go. To provide for this there are usually a sufficient number of priests available. In the private confession the priest may either give the absolution there to the penitent or wait until everyone is assembled outside. Then all the priests give absolution in unison, which absolution applies only to those who have confessed. Because communal confession is new to most areas there are no specific directives from Rome. Variations will be evident in certain areas. Most places that do have these celebrations explicitly forbid general absolution; that is, mass absolution for all those assembled whether they went into the private confessional or not. The priests in unison may give absolution together to the assembly, but, as indicated before, only to those who actually went to confession.

Before this absolution there is, in some places, the common recitation of a penance. After all is over, the assembly departs singing some joyous song of praise and thanksgiving.

There are already some of these communal celebrations being printed and more will follow. One is *Celebrations of Penance* by Francis Gross, S. J., put out by the Catholic Action Office, Notre Dame, Indiana. There is a fully explained sample listed in the appendices of this book. Several dioceses have already taken the initiative. Here, for example, are two paragraphs from the directives put out by the Diocese of Madison, Wisconsin, in a letter of June 13, 1969:

> . . . Throughout the Catholic world there has emerged what is called the Community or Communal Penance Service.
>
> The Liturgical Commission of the Diocesan Priests Senate has studied this matter and developed a set of guidelines for the proper use of this communal celebration of Penance. . . . Until such time as the general law of the Church includes a more complete and explicit guidance for this newly developed form I herewith announce and confirm that all communal Penance services in the Diocese of Madison are to be guided by the directives contained in the enclosed guidelines prepared by the Liturgical Commission. . . .

The Bishop then hastens to add the caution:

> In order to avoid all confusion in this matter, we forcefully remind all priests in the Diocese of Madison that so-called "general absolution," or absolution given publicly to one or many, without prior confession of grave sins, both as to number and kind, is absolutely forbidden and a direct violation of the regulations now governing communal Penance Celebrations. The permission and directives that priests in union may confer absolution on the reassembled community is not general absolution because the priests who are giving the absolution may lawfully give it only to those penitents who have already confessed to them.

Confession, then, is undergoing some changes; not indeed in its essential form but in its externals. These externals are meant to recover our lost perspectives; that sin is a saying 'no' to a friend, that sin offends the whole Christ, that sin should be apologized for within that very same christian assembly that we have offended. Changes then both within the system of private confession and within the format of any communal service celebration should not alarm us. The reality of sincere sorrow and a change of heart carry the same force. It is only that the sacrament must be extended and revised to display these truths in greater depth. Again we repeat the words of Vatican II in the decree on the liturgy: "The rite and formulas for the sacrament of penance are to be revised so that they may more clearly express the nature and the effect of the sacrament" (no. 72).

IX

A Brief History
of Confession

1

At this point it might be well in a short chapter to give a
brief outline of the long and varied practices of confession. We have indicated already in previous chapters some
changes in approaches and the introduction of the present
day novelty of communal confessions. We quoted the Vatican Council as saying that the rites and formulas of penance
are to be revised. Poschmann in his scholarly work, *Penance
and the Anointing of the Sick,* says that the Church does remain free to determine the form of confession. Let us then
take a look at an outline—and it can only be an outline in the
light of past history and from the decrees of the Council of
Trent—of the historical facts that could lead Poschmann to
make his remarks.

In going back over the records of the past two thousand
years we find that there is no explicit reference to confessional format as we know it before the third or fourth centuries. This is not entirely to be wondered at. After all, these

were the beginnings of Christianity and the era of persecution. Fervor was high and with such preoccupations the emphasis was not on sin and repentance formulas as such. Also, like so many other truths, sin and repentance in themselves were simply accepted as a normal part of the life of the average Christian and needed no specific references and no special publicity as to manner and procedure. Yet, even if details are lacking

> Literature from the immediate postapostolic period shows that the Church continued to be aware of its power to forgive sin. Already in the Didache, which may antedate some of the New Testament writings, forgiveness of sins is mentioned in connection with the Eucharist. Both Clement of Rome and Ignatius of Antioch, writing at the turn of the first century A.D., connect forgiveness of sins with the jurisdiction possessed by bishops. The earliest Christian writers state quite clearly that sin will be pardoned no matter how great the malice, provided the person genuinely wants to return to Christ and the Church (Bernard Cooke, *Christian Sacraments and Christian Personality*, p. 85).

With the third and fourth centuries came certain heresies and these heresies, as always, provoked both publicity and precision on doctrinal matters and practice. This was the case in reference to the treatment accorded to sin and forgiveness. One of the most intriguing developments of these centuries, however, has given Church historians and theologians a problem. It is the problem, not yet fully solved or understood, of "unicity." This word means "only once" or "single-timeness" and it seems clear that the Church had the practice during these centuries of forgiving certain sins only once: adultery, idolatry and murder. Once a person committed these sins, confessed them and did penance there was no second chance for forgiveness if these sins were committed again. This certainly was a harsh practice. There was even criticism of the pope because of his willingness to forgive some other grave sins. Tertullian for one disagreed with the more lenient policy of the bishop of Rome. Others were inclined to refuse sacramental pardon until the moment of death. Such practices startle us, yet they undoubtedly existed. But they existed in practice and were matters of discipline; they were never a matter of doctrine. In theory the forgiveness of all sins could be had not only once but "70 times 7." In the *Apostolic Tradition* of Hippolytus (4th century) the text for the consecration of a bishop mentions his authority "according to thy commands to loose every bond according to the authority that thou gavest to the apostles." Still, the harshness was in vogue at this time.

This rigorism began to wane somewhat in the fifth and sixth centuries. For example, St. John Chrysostom who died in 408 introduced a more merciful sentiment. He wrote:

> . . . If you are a fornicator, or an adulterer, if you are an extortioner or greedy, come to the Church that you may learn to do these things no more . . . this I tell you every day.

Some of his contemporaries did not go for this softening and they condemned John, horrified that he "holds out pardon for sinners by teaching the following: If you shall sin a second time, do penance a second time, and as often as you shall sin, come to me and I shall cure you." Yet this more lenient attitude was beginning to find its way from Rome itself. A pope of the time, Innocent I, although still holding to the old rigorist attitude, said that reconciliation should take place again at the hour of death.

The upshot of all this was the natural reaction on the part of the people to postpone penance until death. After all, if certain sins could be forgiven only once why not wait until one was dying and clear the slate altogether? Penance thus became associated with dying. Not only that, but rather severe penalties were given for sins. In fact so harsh were some penalties that this too led people to put off receiving penance until death time. Even the great St. Ambrose, with his grasp of human nature, urged the young men to put off going to confession until all their wild oats were sown.

All in all, it seems that in practice people were left to their own devices and the use of official confessing and doing penance was neglected until the time of death.

There is one more brief item we should mention in these early centuries. In the fourth and fifth centuries public confession was in vogue. This does not mean that people shouted their sins in front of everybody (although some did) but rather approaching confession was a public act and doing the penalties was a public event as was the final reconciliation. In fact, the whole christian community was involved and prayed for the penitent. In the last chapter we have seen a revival of such a community involvement in the introduction of the communal confessions.

Were there no strictly private confessions in the early centuries as we know them today? There is some record that private confessions were existent but the data on this point is not too clear. Yet Father Cooke says, "Documents from the time of St. Augustine and Pope Leo I definitely distinguish between the private confession of sins made to the bishop and the public performance of the assigned penance." Even so, private confessions as such seem to have been considered an abuse and were not an active part of early Christianity. In summary we can quote Father Riga in his survey from his book *Sin and Penance:*

> . . . It is enough to say that during this whole period of the fifth and sixth centuries, canonical penance alone was recognized as official in the Church. In practice, however, this penance was restricted to a very small number of Christians because of the rigors involved. It was considered as a direct preparation for death, not as the ordinary remedy for sin during life. These and other odious demands of the penitential discipline made penance objectionable for the great majority of Christians. From a pastoral point of view, the situation was extremely confusing and inefficacious. It is with these perspectives in mind that we can better understand the innovations of the seventh and eighth centuries (p. 102).

2

Yes, the seventh and eighth centuries did bring some refreshing changes. These changes were largely due to the Irish monks who came to the mainland. They were innovators on the mainland because life in their native Ireland was different and thus elicited different responses in religious life. For example, there were no large cities in Ireland at the time and the Church as a result consisted of a widespread group of monasteries. In each locale the abbot and the monks were the center of religious life and a more family atmosphere was evident in relationship to the people. This paternal rapport spilled over into the people's specifically sacramental life where penance came to be administered in a private manner between spiritual child and father. The priest-monk not only heard the confessions in private but provided private penalties and effected the private reconciliation between penitent and God. The more public and canonical procedures had not come over from the mainland to disturb this arrangement. This was not to say that the monks were lenient. They could and did give rather severe penalties and provided harsh remedies; but they did effectively eliminate the more terrifying features connected with confessions elsewhere. In a word, the Irish monks were practicing private confession much the same as we know it today. Moreover, since confession was a private affair it could be received more than once. This factor alone was to give great relief to the people and thus it was not long in spreading when at last the monks made their way to the continent and introduced this form of confession. In essence, of course, all of the official, canonical elements remained: the telling of the sins, the Church sitting in judgment in the person of the monk, the penalty and reconciliation—but all was now done through the priest-representative of both Church and community.

In the old penitential books there are listed not only some fairly harsh penalties for sin but some rather beautiful formulas and preambles to confession. Just before the Council of Trent and thereafter action and word were quite reduced and we have lost much of the surrounding ceremony and word that accompanied the sacrament. In fact, a minimal formula of absolution, until recently in Latin, has replaced some lovely prayers.

Later centuries brought certain deletions and additions. After Trent a more legal approach was specified for confession: the careful enumeration of kind and number, the carefully defined five steps that most present day adults learned. Even before Trent the so-called "confession of devotion" came into vogue. That is, people confessed venial sins even though this was never strictly required and could be forgiven outside of confession or they went to confession for spiritual advice and direction. Right up to the Middle Ages it was the predominant view that in case of necessity one must and could confess even to a layman! St. Ignatius of Loyola, the founder of the Jesuits, held this view. The confessions of children, about which we shall speak in the next chapter, did not appear until at least the ninth century. The confessional box as we know it did not appear until after the Council of Trent in the sixteenth century. Father Karl Rahner in his essay "Problems Concerning Confession" (*Theological Investigations*, Vol. III) summarizes the long history of confession this way:

> But St. Joseph did not build the first confessional. There were many centuries when there was no confession of devotion. St. Augustine never went to confession. There were centuries when the saintly bishops of Gaul preached that one should *do* penance but go to confession only on one's death-bed. There were Councils which warned against administering this sacrament to a young person in danger of death, since he might recover and might then find the life-long penitential obligations far too difficult. There were centuries during which ecclesiastical reconciliation could be received only *once*. . . . It was not until the thirteenth century that there appeared the indicative formula of absolution and that a beautiful penitential liturgy was permitted to shrink to bare absolution. . . . During twelve or rather thirteen centuries the Church managed without the explicit distinction (which seems of such capital importance to us) between perfect and imperfect contrition . . . (p. 191).

One conclusion of this brief summary gives credence to Poschmann's words referred to at the beginning of this chapter: that the Church remains quite free to determine the form of confession. As true as this is as a varied penitential history shows, we must note what has remained constant. We must note that the basic elements of contrition, reconciliation and satisfaction have always been present while the form has undergone change. We must expect this. After all, the Church is living and dynamic as is Christ himself. The Church suits herself to the needs of the people and that is why she has changed in her approaches to confession and can and will change again. The history of penance in fact has not only allowed much leeway in the past but has thereby laid the groundwork for further directions for the future.

X

First Confession
for Children

1

In recent years much has been written on the age of confession for children. There are those who maintain that the traditional age of seven and the time just prior to First Holy Communion should be maintained. Others say that a child below the age of eleven or twelve is really not capable of committing sin and so confession should be postponed until then, leaving First Communion to be made at the normal time. One noteworthy example of this latter is the well publicized directive of Bishop Petrus Moors in the Netherlands who on May 15, 1964, permitted the raising of the age for first confession in his diocese.

The question of what age children should receive their first confession is not an easy one and will be debated for a long time to come. Notable names in theology line up on either side of the question. It is important to begin therefore with the caution that polarization of this question is not necessary. It should never become a question of whether

Johnny or Suzy *must* make first confession at seven or eleven but rather, whatever age is chosen, it should be a question of the best possible preparation and insight for this or that child. In this chapter I shall give the reasons for postponing the age of confession since we are all familiar with the current traditional age and therefore it might be well to see the reasoning by the advocates of change.

Perhaps the general theme and rationale for the postponement of confession is given best by two authors, Robert P. O'Neil and Rev. Michael A. Donovan, in their article "The Question of Preadolescent Sin" (*Insight:* Quarterly Review of Religion and Mental Health, Vol. 4, Spring 1966, pp. 1-10). I shall rely heavily on this paper in this chapter. They say:

> It is our firm belief that good psychology and good morality cannot be in conflict. It must be made clear from the start that preadolescent children are unquestionably capable of doing wrong: they can commit acts which are forbidden, omit those which are required, know what they are doing, expect punishment, and feel guilt and remorse. This is not, however, mature moral consciousness. Rather, their understanding of right and wrong has a ceiling imposed by the level of cognitive development. They are incapable of interpreting or evaluating their actions in a morally culpable way. The attainment of certain crucial concepts and the exercise of autonomy of judgment do not occur until the onset of adolescence, i.e., between eleven and thirteen years of age in most children. Until that time, they can be guilty of only material, not formal wrong.

This last distinction between "material" and "formal" wrong is one we made earlier in the book when we said that not every wrong-doing is a sin. Wrong-doing is an objective happening but sin becomes involved only when the person brings his full knowledge, insight and consent to bear on it. These authors would maintain that children, below eleven, simply do not have the intellectual capacity and insightful potential to commit sin. Wrong-doing they can do with alarming regularity, but the capacity for genuine sin is simply not there. The realization quotient of children is too low to allow for a mature concept of sin.

The authors fall back on Thomas Aquinas. This great theologian teaches that one cannot commit a venial sin before he is capable of committing a mortal sin. Since children cannot commit mortal sins then they cannot commit venial ones and therefore need not go to confession. Children are not capable of mortal sin because the general concept of mortal sin as a severed friendship with Him, as a rejection of God as friend and one's final end is too sophisticated for them. Such large insights and wide concepts as "final end," everlasting friendship, long-term relationship with the Father, deviation from one's final orientation—these are simply foreign to the preadolescent mind. The child has not reached the intellectual level where such concepts mean anything or have any content.

Again, children can do actions which are wrong and seriously so and give consent to wrong doing and this predisposes them to commit real sin in later life, but such so-called "sins" can only be materially wrong on the outside and not reprehensible on the inside to the level of positive sinning. In fact, the wrongness of any child's acts does not rest on any intellectual insight but rather flows from his own concrete relationships to his parents, teachers, brothers or sisters or playmates. Or else he reacts to pleasure-pain motivations. There is not any moral decision involved. His actions have only an immediate reference to Mommy's or Daddy's frown or smile, hug or threat; his playmates' applause or jeers, his teachers' A+ or D−.

That children cannot commit venial sin before they can commit mortal sin is taught not only by St. Thomas but also by some of his major commentators. Father Martin McCabe, O. P., for example, says:

> The discussion of the impossibility of venial sin being present in one who has only original sin leads St. Thomas to an analysis of the beginnings of thought-life in man. Before one arrives at the age of discernment, when he can see the distinction between good and evil or what is called the use of reason, he cannot commit a sin of any kind, and cannot have venial sin in his soul. . . .

The theologian Billuart says:

> . . . In order to perform free acts which are morally indifferent there must be an understanding of the harmony or disharmony between one's acts and the rules of morality, which is not had unless there be perfect use of reason.

Bernard Haring in his book *Shalom* says:

> The most rigid opinion would maintain that after ten years, children are capable of mortal sin. As I said before, I doubt if the average child of eleven, twelve or thirteen can commit a mortal sin (p. 281).

All of these comments come down to this: for any kind of sin moral thinking and moral insight are required. The preadolescent child does not have this kind of thinking or insight and so theologically he cannot commit sin of any kind, grave or venial. He can do all kinds of wrong and he can be quite aware of his wrong-doing, but he just doesn't have the intellectual equipment to commit an insightful sin. There-fore, incapable of sin of any degree the preadolescent does not need to go to confession. Confession should be postponed until early adolescence in order for the child to benefit from it.

Of course, what has confused many is the Church's prac-tice of hearing the children's confessions at the age of seven, just before First Holy Communion. Pope Pius X is respon-sible for fixing this "age of reason." In his decree on com-munion of August 8, 1910, he established for the universal Church the practice of having children go to confession and communion at the age of seven. He was, of course, working on the assumption that children could commit sin at any age. Previous history of the sacrament of penance, as we have seen in the last chapter, tells us that children's confessions were not heard at all until the eighth or ninth centuries. When seven was settled on it was concluded to be the "age of reason" a phrase which in itself has an uneven history and has varied in the past anywhere from seven to fourteen or fifteen.

Still, in contrast to the theological arguments just put forth, St. Thomas also teaches that once a person *begins* to enjoy the use of reason, grave and consequently venial sin are not to be entirely excluded as possibilities. The great moral theologian, St. Alphonsus Liguori, held that if a child can know even in a quite rudimentary fashion that God is offended by a certain act and if that child is sorry and has some purpose of amendment, he can be absolved.

2

From the theological arguments for postponing the age of confession let us look at some psychological and liturgical considerations. The great Swiss psychologist Piaget has done a great deal of noted work on the intellectual development of children and, in his research, has amassed a great deal of evidence to show that the full and perfect use of reason does not appear until about eleven or twelve years of age at the earliest. Until this age children's thought processes tend to be generally self-centered and self-measured, very concrete as opposed to abstract, nonrelational to other schemes and syncretic; that is, children under 12 tend to group bits of reality into no definable pattern: one reality latches on to another like a patch work quilt without an emerging unity or logical grouping. This syncretic thinking process, Piaget found, persists until 11 or 12 and does tend to hinder the comprehension of abstract concepts. In fact, the younger the child, the more concrete the thinking. Piaget stated ". . . a simple relationship like that of brother still presented insurmountable difficulties to the child of 9-10." In intelligence tests the emphasis shifts from the concrete to the abstract at about 11 to 13 years of age. It seems that a child has to reach a certain age before he can really move upward to abstract thought and principles and therefore into the realm of moral judgment and sin-decision.

O'Neil and Donovan go on to comment:

> One may argue at this point that the exceptional or precocious child, because of his accelerated mental development, should be capable of mature moral acts and judgments at a significantly earlier age than the average. If this were true, it would nevertheless apply to only a small fraction of the population. In fact, however, the results of research on moral development, political thinking, and the development of autonomy of judgment, to be discussed next, reveal that even high I.Q. cannot overcome the developmental obstacle;

and that age, maturation, and experience are far more determining than is intelligence in the development of the capacity for moral acts.

In his book, *Youth: The Years from Ten to Sixteen*, Gesell observes:

> The ten year old is just beginning to distinguish between right and wrong. . . . Characteristically, Ten is concretely specific. . . . He is somewhat naively susceptible to ethical teaching, and over-reacts to it with what resembles a self-righteous attitude. In these various patterns of behavior, Ten displays transparently the persistence of childhood characteristics—the concreteness of his "moral" orientation and the simplicity of dependence shown toward his mother. With adolescence there will be reorientations, but in general they will be gradual rather than precipitous, and they will be governed by the growth of social intelligence and new attitudes toward his peers.

Thus modern psychology would seem to back up the theological arguments: the preadolescent child is incapable of committing sin, either grave or venial. His various "wrong-doings" are just that: materially bad actions without the necessary intellectual insight relating means and ends to make such actions truly moral. Since the child cannot commit sin, there is no need for confession as a means of remitting sin.

As for liturgical considerations, following the suggestions of Klemens Tilmann (*Making Sense of Confession*, edited Otto Betz, Franciscan Herald Press, 1968, Chicago, Illinois) we can enumerate other reasons for postponing the child's confession. First of all, there is the question of the new emphasis on the meal aspect of the Mass: that the Mass is the sacrificial banquet of the faithful where fraternity and community are fostered. Around the altar and by sharing the common food (eucharist) the christian community is strengthened and informed with charity. All family members have the right to participate in the christian family meal (Mass)—and this includes the children as soon as they are able to sit at the table as it were. The analogy to one's own family experience should be obvious. The child is kept in the high chair as long as this is needed. But there comes the day when he is old enough to sit at the table on a regular chair and eat the same food and partake in the same family spirit as anyone else. So, too, when the christian child is able, he should take part in the christian family meal and be permitted to take part in the common eucharistic food for he now belongs to the family table. This is normal and natural. But confession is extraordinary in the sense that it reconciles the sinner to God and the community in order to make him worthy of the eucharistic table. But, as we have seen, such a procedure is not needed for the innocent child. He needs no reconciliation. He hasn't separated himself yet from God or God's table. Liturgically then, confession should not be a part of the child's approach to the communion table. There is no connection for him, no necessity.

Secondly, we must admit that a child needs proof of love much much earlier than a realization of his own sins. He should experience love before he can ever learn what forgiveness means. It is by sharing with joy at the family table of the Lord first that he will someday realize what he has forsaken. To teach him companionship-love, then, would seem liturgically and psychologically a better long term preparation for confession in the future—and so it is wise to let him receive the family food (communion) first.

Thirdly, separating confession from communion will eliminate the dreadful connection the people have so often made between confession and communion. "You must go to confession before you can receive communion" has been uttered by really pious people who frequently absented themselves from the eucharistic table on its reasoning. For some people, the false connection is never broken. Separating these sacraments from the beginning in the minds of the children should leave them free to approach the table of the Lord with single-minded devotion rather than with apprehension that they didn't go to confession.

An offshoot of this error is the feeling that, therefore, one must be 'perfectly pure and worthy' before approaching Holy Communion. But this is not true. We must, of course, be as prepared as possible, but being prepared need not mean and cannot mean perfection: what is needed is humbleness of attitude in acknowledging that we are sinners approaching the *forgiving* Lord, "the Lamb, who takes away the sins of the world." "True reverence for the Eucharist does not demand purity from venial sins," says Klemens Tilmann, "for here 'the work of salvation is accomplished.'" In fact, the Council of Trent says about the Mass that "this sacrifice is a real sacrifice of atonement, it brings it about that we may receive mercy and find grace for timely help." Of communion itself, the Council went on to say that this food has been instituted "as an antidote which frees us from our daily trespasses." From this point of view, to try to be "perfect" in order to receive Holy Communion does not make sense. Rather we approach "imperfectly" to find a remedy for our spiritual ills. That this approach is sound is backed up by the historical fact, mentioned before, that during the first eight centuries of Christianity no child *ever* went to confession before his first communion.

Still, others would maintain that sorrow for personal sin is essential for a meaningful participation in the Mass and for the reception of Holy Communion. They hold that theology teaches that the sacrament of penance prepares an individual for union with Christ and his mystical members in communion. They point to St. Paul, for example, who says that a man should first examine himself lest he eat the bread or drink the cup unworthily. If such confessional sentiments are enjoined as a preamble to Mass and communion, then this also should include the children who are encouraged to attend Mass at an early age. Monsignor Poschmann says that confession "is clearly most appropriate before the celebration of the Eucharist, because communal liturgical prayer also calls for a preliminary purification of conscience" (p. 22).

3

Considerations from experience and common sense are further offered for the postponing of children's confessions until a later date. Proponents of postponement say that the danger of legalism is thereby minimized. We've seen legalism before. It is trying to manipulate God by observing all of the rules yet not commit oneself to Him personally. It's getting preoccupied with all of the externalisms of humanity and religion and leaving aside "the weightier matters of justice and love." In confession legalism means a tit-for-tat with God, a bargaining with Him: "I'll tell my sins and you give me absolution." People sometimes rush into the confessional with just that attitude. This habit is often acquired in childhood where the child has little or nothing to tell and even invents some sins; and this is a habit difficult to overcome. It is better to wait until the child is older and can be trained into a more personal relationship with the Father than to have him mechanically go to confession for many years before maturity.

There are priests who can testify that, by and large, the average youngster neither understands what nor why he is confessing. His figures are often astronomical and amusing. "This is one month since my last confession, I missed Mass twelve times." Such a child may be absolutely sincere but his mathematics leave something to be desired. Children's concept of the degree of seriousness of what they did is often betrayed by their tone of voice. "I dish-obeyed my mommy", is said matter-of-factly. There's a more solemn tone to "I dish-obeyed my daddy." Disobedience is the main sin. But children can climb the scale. Much more serious, for example, is "I hit the dog!"—more serious, anyway, than hitting one's sister or brothers; presumedly they are fair game. And, finally, there is the "ultimate sin" for which they are not sure they will ever receive absolution, "I went to the bathroom outside!" With such comments from the small fry, it's no wonder that for many priests, hearing the confessions of children is engaging in a kind of Art Linkletterism. In a more serious vein, it suggests that children's capacity to make true moral judgments is quite absent.

Some would object that postponing confession would deprive the children of an avenue of grace. The answer given to this objection is that the end does not justify the means. If children cannot sin, there is no need to go to confession. Besides, they can and should go to Holy Communion if they wish to grow in grace—something which they apparently did for the first eight or nine hundred years of Christianity anyway.

There are those who are anxious to maintain the traditional early confession on the premise that it inculcates this habit into the children: the sooner they start the more in-grained the habit of frequent confession can become. Others refute this from ordinary, everyday experience. They point to all of the decades where Catholic boys and girls were mar-shalled over to church for first Thursday confessions and led back again on First Fridays for Mass and communion. This system still persists in many parishes today. Yet for all of the multitude of children who went through and still go through this routine, there is this basic pastoral question: where are they the first Thursdays of July and August and September. Rather, in October it is the familiar, "Bless me, Father, I have sinned. It has been three months since my last confession." Moreover, there is no evidence that this "habit" has held up with present day adults. By and large such rote training does not take.

There are one or two more points that proponents of later confession for children make. They claim that too early con-fession tends to make confession a substitute for personal initiative. It tends to an unhappy paternalism whereby the child grows up leaning on the priest for decisions he should make himself; it tends to see confession as a moral backstop in an emergency and thus sap the risk and adventure of giv-ing one's all to God. Further, there is, they say, the possibility of producing scrupulosity in a child with too early confession. He should not be preoccupied with sin and running to fre-quent confession. He may set himself up for the possibility of thinking of God in terms of the "Mean Auditor," a kind of Super Policeman who is waiting to chastise every fault and who wants an accounting of every deed. A child may never feel quite at home with such an all-seeing deity. He may never be able to satisfy the demands of such a strict majesty. He may never be able to apologize enough to such a haughty accountant. In a word, he may become scrupulous. On the other hand again, others say that scrupulosity is a home problem and starts there and that children can be trained to run with joy to their Father's knee rather than to fear Him or retreat into scrupulosity.

Keeping in mind the comments of dissent, let us now put into summary the main points put forth for the postponement of first confession for children:

1. Theologically, a child cannot commit venial sin until he is capable of committing a grave sin. But this latter requires a certain level of intellectual and cognitive development which simply does not come to the ordinary child until he is at least 12 or 13.

2. Up to this early adolescent time children's thinking is quite egocentric, nonlogical, concrete and nonrelational; the opposite elements, however, are needed for grave sin.

3. The development of true intellectual insight comes with later age. Modern psychology, in fact, demonstrates that cognitive development needed for a genuine mature moral judgment comes about 12 to 14 years of age.

4. Therefore, children really can't be guilty of grave, insightful sin. They can do a lot of wrong things, know what they're doing and feel sorry—but this is not the level of grave sin. Thus, confession is not needed.

5. Further, postponing confession leaves room for the child to grow into the "family" spirit by partaking first of the Christian family meal of the Eucharist.

6. By receiving communion first the child learns the intimacy of the Father's love and friendship; later con-

cepts of sin can then be best seen in terms of that friendship wounded or broken.

7. Postponing confession can prevent undue legalism in the child's approach to God.
8. It can sever the undesirable connection between the two sacraments of confession and communion.
9. It will defer any undue concept of God forbidding and lessen the possibility of incurring scrupulosity.
10. Postponing confession should in no way deter any healthy habits of frequenting the sacrament in later life.

In conclusion we must repeat that the matter of the time of children's confessions is by no means settled. Not all agree with postponing confessions to a later time. Others are experimenting with different age groups. Still others are introducing children to confession in a communal confession situation. In all of this, the comment made at the beginning of this chapter still holds: there is no need to polarize the question. It is not a question of a child making his first confession at twelve or seven or not at all. At this point, rather, whatever is done, should be done with caution, with the greatest sensitivity in starting the child on the right road to a truly mature relationship with his best friend.

XI

Formula and Examination

1

Everyone knows how to begin his confession. "Bless me, Father, for I have sinned." But how many realize the full implications of that word "bless"? To bless means to rejoice, to congratulate, to be happy. What we are saying is, "Be happy with me, Father." This immediately raises the question of how Father could possibly be happy when the penitent finishes up with, "for I have sinned." But obviously the call to happiness is not over one's sinning, but that one is there at all. Congratulations are in order because this human being has finally acknowledged the one truth about himself about which he can be sure: he is a sinner and he needs God's saving grace. No confessor would ever contradict this attitude for it is basic to salvation. The penitent is one of a long line of sinners throughout the ages who have fallen to the ground in acknowledgement of his guilt before the Father. He is obeying the God who said in the Old Testament: "If a man or woman commits any of the sins by which men

123

break faith with Yahweh, that person . . . must confess that sin" (Numbers 5:6-7). He is following the words of Jesus who warned that unless a man had a true change of heart (*metanoia*) he could not enter the kingdom of heaven. No wonder, then, we begin with a note of joy. And who cannot see in this an echo of that father who told his neighbors to rejoice with him because his prodigal son who was dead had come back to life.

If we regain this full meaning of our opening formula we shall enter the confessional with a new spirit. By the same token, however, there is no need to be confined to this formula. Adults and children alike are free and indeed encouraged to make up their own that may suit the occasion and their own sentiments. Here are some examples from adults and children:

> "Rejoice with me Father, I wish to come back to the People of God."

> "Congratulate me, Father, I have come to be reconciled to the Christian community."

> "Bless me, Father, for I want to be taken back into the Family of God."

> "Father, I am here to confess my sins to the entire Church."

> "Celebrate with me Father; I am here to acknowledge both my sinfulness and my need for Christ, my Savior."

These and similar formulas are good because they force a person to be creative and this creativity should lead him to a better understanding of just what it is he is about to do. It also tells the priest that this penitent has taken the trouble to give a further dimension to his approach to Christ in the sacramental encounter; the priest will pick up the cue and feel free to talk to the penitent on a similar level. He may also be inclined to give a penance beyond the usual three Hail Marys since he perceives that this is a person who would be ready for this.

What might the priest tell such a person for penance? He might have him go home and recite Psalm 50, David's cry of penitence. He may have him read something from the Bible, say, the story of the Prodigal Son. He may have him do nothing more arduous than give a compliment to his wife before the week is out or do nothing except for the next three minutes after he leaves the confessional to kneel before the church crucifix and simply look at it. There are many penances the priest would and could give and readily does to those who give him some hint of readiness. He usually does wait for some indications of confessional sophistication because he has likely been frustrated too many times before by people who simply could not break out of the "Three Hail Marys" pattern. After urging some man to drop a few pennies in the poor box or some woman to make her husband's favorite dessert by way of apology for the argument she mentioned the priest is met with, "Yes, Father, but what is my penance?" In desperation he says, "Three Hail Marys," and gives up trying to educate the penitents to something more varied and meaningful.

2

With what we have seen in general in this book we know now that we must approach our examination of conscience in a new light before entering the confessional. We must, for one thing, stop confessing mere wrong-doings that are not sins. We must stop confessing items that really don't matter at all and really have no bearing on our lives. Rather, in our examination of conscience we must be more penetrating and really get to know ourselves and our spiritual progress. I might suggest three broad areas of examination. There are other areas and there are some excellent adult examination of conscience booklets. Some suggested examination for children and for adults is given in the appendices of this book. Let us now look at the three categories and give sample confessions in each of them.

First a penitent might examine himself in the area of *vocation*. Each person has one particular vocation. One man is a doctor, another an accountant. One woman is a housewife, another a receptionist. Whatever their state in life, such people can grow in holiness in it, can bring their christian witness to it. We could ask ourselves some basic question in the area of vocation. Do I do my work well? Do I cheat in my work or try to get by on another's labor? How do I treat my fellow workers? What do I contribute to office spirit or factory spirit? Children can ask themselves: Do I constantly copy homework? What do I contribute to class spirit? Housewives can ask about their chores at home and obligations to keep the house running well. But, beyond this general vocation status, there is the larger and more basic vocation to Christian generosity: questions concerning one's attitude, one's willingness to give a little more than strictly required, one's role as peacemaker, deflector of anger, rerouter of the malicious gossip, sign of forgiveness. There are questions of one's prayer life and sincere desire to help others; questions of motivations behind our actions. This whole area of vocation is simply one of God's will. This vocation of mine is so much a part of my life: how do I live it?

The next area of examination is *charity*. What do I do about the person I really don't like and who, as a matter of fact, is so unlikable? Do I at least pray for him or her? Do I ever think of the other families, those without one spouse or another, the poor and discriminated? How about talking harmfully against another? Do I make fun of another's defects, color or nationality? What about questions of justice? There are many things I cannot do, yet there are some ways I can help my neighbor. My town or parish may not be up to par in christian commitment, but is that because I have left the field to others who perhaps care less than I? How about at home? Have I ever really apologized *first* to my husband or wife before I went to confession to be reconciled with my Father and the Church? Do I translate my love into small actions: the favor done, the compliment paid, the courtesy rendered? When was the last time I expressly said to my spouse, "I love you"? Am I trying to run my life of love according to a few strict and negative rules or do I make an effort to respond to the urging of the Holy Spirit? Do I measure myself on the criterion of Christ? Would Jesus do this? This whole area of charity is not running down the Ten Commandments to see if we have killed anyone lately, but the inner probing of genuinely loving one's neighbor according to the inspirations of the Holy Spirit.

A third area that we might examine ourselves in is *omission*. This is a negative variation of the area of charity. This examination centers around the things left undone; things that, as a follower of Christ, I ought to have done. Oh, there was no glaring and obvious grave sin apparent, but there was nevertheless a real omission of charity. "I could have helped my wife with the dishes, but I didn't." "I could have been nicer to that person, but I wasn't." "I could have volunteered for that job, but I was too lazy." There are all those semiconscious lost oportunities that float in our mind: the smile unsmiled, the pat on the back not given, the tender word unspoken, the act of kindness undone.

Under these three headings can come all of the other questions of faith and religion. Questions as to whether faith was really a factor in buying this new car or deciding to have or not to have another child. Questions as to where that better swim club really fits in to our lives, whether moving to this or that neighborhood will enrich our Christian commitment. Questions of purity and modesty as seen against the background of loving my neighbor. Questions of truthfulness and anger seen in the context of love.

In addition to such positive areas of self-examination we should try, as much as we can, to give the reasons for our failures. There are times when we no doubt deceive ourselves, but in general this procedure is most helpful. Here are some examples:

A school boy: "Bless me, Father, I am a nine-year-old boy in the sixth grade. I have come to be reconciled to Jesus and the community. It's been two months since my last confession. Twice I copied my homework because I was too lazy to do it myself. I wasn't very helpful to the class spirit a couple of times and I fooled around in class and kept the other kids from learning because I didn't want to pay attention myself. There's this kid in school that's not very popular and I could have gone over to talk to him but I was afraid that the other kids would make fun of me, so I didn't. I knew my mother had a headache and I could have minded my little sister, but I didn't because I wanted to play ball. I was watching television instead of helping my mother with the dishes."

A high school girl: "Rejoice with me, Father. I am a high school girl. I want to be a better member of God's family.

It's been three weeks since my last confession. Well, there's this girl in school who's sort of different. She is Puerto Rican or something and the other girls don't bother with her too much. A couple of times I was going to go over and speak to her but I didn't. I guess I failed in omission. I left out a christian love that I should have given and for this I am sorry. Also, I did my homework a little sloppily. I talked about some other girls; and I was going to give some money in the poor box but I spent it on myself instead. I'm sorry for not being a better Christian and I ask you to take me back into the community."

Before we go on with other examples, let us notice a few things. First, let me assure you that children and adolescents are quite capable of making confessions given in the examples. We have trained them to this and they respond quite wonderfully. Notice, too, the attempt to get behind the sins, the reasons why they did or did not do certain things. You will notice that, strictly speaking, there are not recorded in these confessions the traditional list of sins, but rather the threefold areas I suggested above. There is one more point worth noting and adopting: the description of their vocational and sexual status: "I am a nine-year-old boy in the sixth grade," "I am a high school girl." This is a highly desirable preamble to the confession. Right away it identifies the kind of person the priest is dealing with and this will obviously make all the difference in the world both as to his advice and to the penance given. So often the priest has trouble even identifying the sexes of the whispered voices. A firm declaration of one's station in life helps greatly and leads the priest to aid in a better confession.

A *housewife:* "Congratulate me, Father, I am here to be reconciled with my Lord and the People of God. I am a housewife and mother of three small children. It's been three months since my last confession. During this time I held a grudge against my husband for about a week. He was wrong and I didn't give him a chance to apologize. My feelings were hurt and I was too preoccupied with that hurt to consider him. We did make up but more because of his efforts than mine. I'm sorry that I didn't give him my forgiveness quicker because I really do love him. Numerous times I was angry with the children. I know that's not a sin—a kind of occupational hazard—but I could have been more responsive to them at the pleasant times, given them a little more of my time. Twice I spoke unkindly of my neighbor. She is a kind of empty-headed person and doesn't grasp things too quickly and I should have been more patient with her and not spoken about her to someone else. I shall try to do some extra kindness for her this week. . . ."

A husband: "Bless me, Father, for I have sinned. This has been six months since my last confession. First of all I've been negligent in getting to confession and this has not been the best example to my children. A couple of times I took part in impure conversation at the office. It's not always easy to avoid these situations but at the same time they know I'm Catholic and I should give some signs that this is not for me or at least walk away. I feel that I wasn't the witness that I should have been. There were some pretty dubious dealings going on in the office; they didn't directly affect me but I was asked about it. Instead of acknowledging the dishonesty I just kept quiet. Once or twice I knew my wife wasn't feeling well and I could have helped with the kids, but I was too preoccupied with my own comfort and I just sat there and read the paper. This is not really loving her as much as I can and I'm sorry for that. I don't always give enough time to my kids. . . ."

These examples give a more sensitive approach to confession. They show the fruit of mature consciences and an awareness of the gospel call to be perfect as the heavenly Father is perfect. Their words are a genuine *sign*, a true outward symbol of their inner sorrow and repentance. Such confessions are true encounters and give every indication that these penitents are approaching Christ with faith.

3

We must close this chapter on formula and examination with two observations. One is the advice that a penitent will normally find it most helpful to go back to the same priest for confession. And if he does this, he or she should inform the priest of this. "Father, I was here last month" or "Father, I've been coming to you regularly for confession." Some people go even further and tell who they are, "Father, this is Mary Smith." There are advantages to this voluntary self-revelation. The priest, like the doctor, can get to know you; he can chart progress and point out paths that only consistent knowledge can give him. The trick is for the penitent to find the right kind of priest and there's no question but each person is perfectly free to go anywhere in the world to find the proper confessor for him.

The second observation is that we must acknowledge that we are human beings and that in our spiritual lives we shall and we must follow the law of gradual progress. In other words, we must be prepared for many confessions, for countless encounters with Christ for no man can declare at any time that he is saved or does not need God anymore. Our human weaknesses will continue at times to overcome us, our need for purification will be constant, our continuous cleansing for a deeper participation in the Eucharist will be obvious. There are no "instant cures." The trouble is that people often become discouraged especially if there is a question of a recurring sin and they will eventually accuse confession of "not working" and that it really "doesn't do me any good." But such people are putting on confession a burden that it is not meant to carry. Confession truly forgives sin but does not take away either the traces in our natures or the persistency of temptation or our own human weaknesses. Confession was never meant to be the final bargain with Christ whereby He bestows impeccability and we no longer have need of Him. Once more Father Evely gets behind the real reason for such an attitude. He says:

> Too often we try to make use of confession itself as a means of doing without God. "Confession doesn't do me any good," one will say, "so I don't go to confession any more." Or another, "It may do me some good, but not much, because I am always confessing the same faults."

> I see what you mean. You would like to use confession as a means of doing without confession. You want to make use of God so that you can do without Him.

> But the main purpose of confession is not a means to acquire moral perfection. It is a religious act, it is the occasion of meeting with the Father, a meeting in which you learn how much He loves you, with what joy and tenderness He pardons you, to what lengths His forgiveness will go, and the wonder of it all.

> Hence it is that you still have before you a handsome future of sins, an attractive future of confession, before you come to know all your weakness, all your ingratitude, and all the mercy of God manifested in that pardon.

> If we were not sinners, with more need for pardon than for bread, we would never know the depths of God's love. Which do you prefer, to be satisfied with yourself, or to be satis-

fied with God? You will go to heaven only as poor persons not because you are content with yourselves, but because you are in admiration of God, happy in being pardoned, astonished at His mercy.

This does not mean that you should always commit the same faults. I believe that when the time comes that you detest your faults less out of pride, when you are willing to be nothing but the opportunity for God to manifest His mercy, in that moment God will grant you a dispensation from sin.

When that time comes, you will know that it is only by His grace that you are preserved, and you will also know that you are always capable of committing sin again. You will feel a fellowship with every sinner, and you will have become capable of assisting them.

XII

"It Is the Lord!"

1

This is the most important chapter in the book because it is about Jesus. We've spent much of the time talking about friendship with God, the broken friendship called sin, our conscience, signs and faith, the community and, finally, the formula and examination of confession. In all of these things, in between the lines as it were, we have been taking for granted one important and vital reality: that none of this—our forgiveness, repentance, restored friendship—would be possible except for God's love in Jesus. *He* invented the sacrament of reconciliation. He made it possible for us to be forgiven, He is the one who forgives. He is merciful. He has the power and majesty to wipe away every sin. He alone has enough love to do this. He is Lord.

In any confessional approach to Christ, it is not our humility, our sincerity, even our sorrow that takes away our sins; it is the freely given and total generosity of the Lord. It is He and none other that gives us the grace to make the approach to begin with; it is He and none other that puts the faith in our hearts and sustains us on our way. He alone is the friend who loves and provides for the friendship-encounter we have come to call the sacrament of reconciliation. Father Rahner reminds us of this when he says:

> Repentance must address itself to Christ, it must be the prayer of the baptized, of a member of the Church, of someone who experiences in himself the saving judgment of the Cross and who knows that salvation can only come from there. The content of the prayer of repentance ought to make it clear to the one who prays that his sins are remitted, not by his repentance as such but by God's grace, that the repentant sinner does not *have* to be forgiven (just because *he* has become better) but that *God* changes the heart and fills it with his Spirit (p. 200).

Keeping this in mind, we must therefore put the emphasis where it belongs: on the Lord. Yet, as I indicated elsewhere in the book, it is possible for some people to go through the whole routine of confession and not actually once think of Christ. Rather, the emphasis is almost totally on ourselves: our sins, our examination, our problems, our waiting in line, our penance, our getting home again. Yet, in proper perspective, we should be crying out to ourselves with joyous anxiety, "It is the Lord!" He is doing "all the work" as it were. It is His blood that redeems, His kindness that has made the moment of encounter possible, His invention of such a sacrament, His bending down to us. We must approach with a deep sense of our nothingness and His might and gracious power. We must approach Him with a realization of the contrast between our weakness and His power, our sins with His holiness, our need with His bounty and our emptiness with His fullness.

But we must go further. We must give the proper term to such an approach. We must suddenly realize that the sacrament of reconciliation, looked at in this way, is *liturgy*. Yes, liturgy; for what is liturgy but the public worship of God and what is an approach such as we have just described but public praise of the Lord? Going thus to confession says in effect, "I am a sinner, nothing. But you, O God, are Lord. You can forgive and heal. You are all. Your power knows no bounds. How great you are, how mighty, how forgiving!" This is worship. That is why Father Haring says in his book *Shalom* that the sacrament of reconciliation is primarily "the liturgical proclamation of the Easter mystery applied here and now to the faithful." Then he adds:

> Confessors and penitents ought to be fully aware that the sacrament of penance is liturgy. Therefore, we have to celebrate the sacrament in a way that focuses attention, not on the sins of the penitent, but totally on the Lord. When we celebrate the sacrament of penance both the confessor and penitent are giving praise to the Lord, especially praise to the merciful Lord.

Penance is the public celebration of what *Jesus* does—and that should be the main attraction of our confession.

Perhaps this is where the old manuals with their list of "sins" were most ineffective. They tended to foster a strictly one-sided view of confession and concentrated almost exclusively on the penitent. The old catechism's preoccupation with the five steps, perfect and imperfect contrition, time, place, circumstance, etc. carried the same fault. Both humanly and theologically speaking all the lists and procedures and repentance in the world would amount to absolutely nothing unless we proclaim, "It is the Lord!"

2

Perhaps nowhere is it more evident that "It is the Lord!" than in the classic story of the prodigal son. It is a tale well known but, for all of that, many of its finer points are missed and frequently a most vital point which bears on this chapter. Since this story is outstanding even as a piece of literature it is presumptuous to try to improve on it. Here we will only attempt to restate it trying to highlight the essential liturgical proclamation it carries.

Here is a father and his two sons running a prosperous farm. The older boy is a gem: serious, conscientious, his father's right hand. But the younger son is unhappy. He feels stifled by the methodical, punctual life on the farm. The work in the fields actually bores him, the smell of the animals irritates him; the whole farm seems like a vast prison where the hired hands are like so many jailers spying on his activities and telling his father. The many young, scatterbrained friends he has in the little neighborhood have filled his head with all kinds of nonsense about life in the big city. In those wonderful and sophisticated places there was gay dining, dancing, music and amazing festivals where at every step he might meet lovely women and pleasant friends instead of his father's loutish farmhands. And all this could be his!

One day the young boy decided that he had had it: he could stand it no longer and made up his mind to do what one of his friends had suggested a long time before. He went to his father and without further ado said to him, "Father, give me the share of property that falls to me." His request was not irregular. According to Hebrew Law, the first born has a right to a double portion. Since there were two sons in this case the younger could expect to receive one third of his father's estate. The father, who knew and loved this son well, must have looked long and sorrowfully into his eyes, but he said nothing; nor did the son have the courage to add a single word to his request. They parted in mutual silence which lasted some days. During this time the settlement was arranged, the property converted into cash and not many days later, the younger son gathered up all his wealth and took a journey into a "far country."

Well, what his friends said was true! What verve and vitality and excitement lay in the big city. Without question he was overcome by the glossy splendor of this "far country." He lost no time in entering into its pleasures and diversions. But, in what has always been a classic situation, there came the day when the slick and crafty city had got all it could from the country bumpkin and he woke up one day to find not only his wallet empty but his newly found friends gone. To add to his utter disillusionment he was forced to face up to one of those frequent famines which plagued the East in those times as well as ours. Hungry and lonely he went to many a house and many a village before someone would give him the job of even minding the pigs. And each day of humiliation and hunger brings back thoughts of his home: his father, his brother, his well-filled plate: why, his father's servants were throwing away more food than they could eat—and tears would fall on the dry grass beside him. At last he could stand it no longer. He said to himself, "Look, no more of this! I will go back home and say that I am sorry, that I am no longer worthy to be called a son, but will be one of the hired hands!" And so he arose, the gospel says, and went to his father.

And now the gospel continues with the most loving, the most wonderful, the most hopeful sentence in the entire bible; a sentence rich with liturgy and endless in depth and hope. "But while he was yet a long way off, his father saw him, and was moved with compassion and ran and kissed him."

Here we must try to picture the vibrant scene that this sentence draws for us. The son has been gone for some months now. Every night after the evening meal the old father walks from the house and stands on the mound in front. He looks hard over the land. His eyes travel over the grass, the fields, the flowers, the orchards, the animals to the windy road. He studies every figure and shadow. He stands there motionless until darkness comes. He strains to get a glimpse of someone. No one comes. He bows his head and returns quietly to the house.

Finally one evening, the father sees a figure in the distance—and he knows immediately! He flings his arms wide open and literally runs over the stoney path, cuts through the field, passes the orchard, catches his robe on a branch and pulls it away ripping it, runs through the hedge and with a last panting dash staggers down the road to embrace the dusty form and kiss the bearded face of his son! Both are in tears. The son tries to say his little rehearsed piece of sorrow, but the father is silencing him with kisses. They walk exhausted and silent back to the house where, with a new vigor, the father orders a celebration for the return of his son for, he says, "my son has returned; he who was dead has been brought back to life!"

What a wonderful story! And now we must see more deeply into it. The first fact we should note is that this is a parable-sermon; no preacher preaches it but Jesus himself, and this is significant because here we have God's view of repentance and confession. And the application of His story is clear as clear can be. *We* are the prodigal children. We have left our Father's house through sin. We have exchanged the virtues and values of home to wallow in the pigsty of selfishness and impurity and uncharitableness and dishonesty. We have left our loving Father for the attractions of a far off country. And yet—yet, how does Jesus picture God? As an avenging Jupiter with the thunderbolt of a punishment in his right hand? This should be the picture. As an angry taskmaster stalking his runaway slave? As a cold cynic leaving us to our own foolishness? No! Jesus says that God, from whose fingertips universes fall, against Whose power the nuclear bomb is as nothing, beside whose beauty Grand Canyon is as a shadow—Jesus says that Almighty God is like a doting father who while his son was yet a long way off, saw him and ran to embrace him. Jesus says that God is like a foolish old man going every night to look for a son who is not there and returning to the house with a heavy heart. Jesus says that God is like that venerable father who did not wait for his son to reach him, but at the first vague sign of the son's return he himself ran and embraced him and showered him with kisses. This, says Jesus, is the kind of God we worship. This is Father and friend.

Thus the focal point of this parable, you see, is not the son: it is the Father. It tells of a Father in heaven who is friend, who "first loved us," who out of the fullness of His heart extends forgiveness. The son in the story can, in essence, only perform liturgy. He can only fall down in numb amazement before such tremendous love and declare truly "it is the Lord!" He can only acknowledge that it is the Father who initiates forgiveness and makes it possible. It is a Father who, while he was yet a long way off, "was moved with compassion and ran . . ." With this in mind, it is no wonder that we desired to look at sin and reconciliation in personal terms, trying to understand that the total experience involves the Father, friend and Lord. In the words of Psalm 102 we are bound to cry out:

> Bless the Lord, O my soul; and all my being, bless his holy name.
> Bless the Lord, O my soul; and forget not all his benefits;
> He pardons all your iniquities, he heals all your ills.

He redeems your life from destruction, he crowns you with goodness and compassion,

He fills your lifetime with good; your youth is renewed like the eagle's—

The Lord performs just deeds and secures the rights of the oppressed.

He has made known his ways to Moses, and his deeds to the children of Israel.

Merciful and gracious is the Lord, slow to anger and abounding in kindness.

He will not always chide, nor does he keep his wrath forever.

Not according to our sins does he deal with us, nor does he requite us according to our crimes.

For as the heavens are high above the earth, so surpassing is his kindness toward those who fear him.

As far as the east is from the west, so far has he put our transgressions from us.

As a father has compassion on his children, so the Lord has compassion on those who fear him,

For he knows how we are formed; he remembers that we are dust.

Man's days are like those of grass; like a flower of the field he blooms;

The wind sweeps over him and he is gone, and his place knows him no more.

But the kindness of the Lord is from eternity to eternity toward those who fear him, and his justice towards children's children

Among those who keep his covenant and remember to fulfill his precepts.—

The Lord has established his throne in heaven, and his kingdom rules over all.

Bless the Lord, all you his Angels, you mighty in strength, who do his bidding, obeying his spoken word.

Bless the Lord, all you his hosts, his ministers, who do his will.

Bless the Lord, all his works, everywhere in his domain. Bless the Lord, O my soul!

3

The parable of the prodigal son also provides us with a good summary of what we have written in this book. It surely involves the concept of personal friendship and sin as that friendship wounded or broken. It shows us the boy's conscience being aware, not that he has strictly done something wrong in leaving his father: after all, it was a mutual agreement—but being aware of the demands of love, of what he ought to have done to and for such a Father. It demonstrates that we have not here the normal telling of sins according to number, kind and circumstance. This is not to say (as we mentioned) that he should and we should not do this. This is to say, rather, that here was a legitimate case of the "abnormal" sign of which we spoke, a sign that was sincere and genuine because it accurately portrayed what was on the inside. Thus we are reminded once more that the burden of approaching the Lord must be, not on the outer mechanics, but on the inner spirit of sorrow and love. Notice, too, the repentance, the willingness "to be converted" (*metanoia*)— "make me as one of your hired hands." Notice, above all, the faith. There was no hesitation or doubt that the father would take him back. He was sure of his father's love as unsure as he was of his own. He approached with faith. Like the other woman in the gospel, he touched the hem of the Lord's garment believing. Finally, notice the community involvement. The community was called in to rejoice and celebrate. There was to be public happiness that one "dead" was restored to the living community because since the community was diminished by the sin of one of its members it should be present too for the enrichment of restoration.

The parable of the prodigal son is thus a whole theology on sin and confession. It is a summary of what we have tried to say in this book. And the wonderful part about it is that it was told by the One who ought to know.

APPENDIX I

Communal Confession Celebrations

As we indicated in the book communal confessions are becoming more popular and some celebrations have been published already and more will come. I would recommend again *Celebrations of Penance*, by Francis Gross, S.J. Basically communal confessions are at present private confessions surrounded with public ceremonies. Usually there are an opening hymn, scripture readings, a sermon, private confessions, public prayers and a final hymn. I have enclosed this sample as one typical of procedure. Remember, there are no official formats yet.

SUGGESTED RITE OF COMMUNAL CONFESSION

It is recommended that the participants assemble in a hall or outside first and have copies of the ceremonies. There should be a cross bearer, two acolytes, a lector to read the Bible reading and one carrying incense. Another person can take the role of commentator to read out the public examination of conscience. All of the people thus involved can be laymen of either sex.

The procession lines up this way: the cross bearer and two acolytes, all of the people involved in the celebration and, at the end of the line, the lector and commentator, the incense bearer and the clergy.

All march two by two into church, the people splitting up by going into the front pews either side of the church. The cross bearer and others go directly into the sanctuary to assigned places. The procedure now takes place as follows:

1. The entrance hymn. This is being sung all the time it takes for the procession to get into church. A penitential hymn like "From the Depths" is recommended.

2. When the others get into the sanctuary, the priest incenses the Bible placed on a lectern by the lector. After the incensation the priest turns to the people and greets them with "The Lord be with you."

   ALL: And with your spirit.

   PRIEST: Let us pray. O Lord, we ask you to enlighten us your servants with the light of your understanding. Cleanse us and make us holy so that we may be able to renew the grace of our baptism. We ask you this through Jesus Christ, our Lord who lives and reigns with you together with the Holy Spirit God, forever and ever. Amen.

3. After this opening prayer, all sit for a reading of the Scripture by the lector. Readings from the Exodus or such New Testament stories as Mary Magdalene, the prodigal son, the lost sheep, etc. are appropriate.

4. After the reading of the Scripture, all sit for a homily.

5. After the homily, all kneel for the following dialogue:

   PRIEST: Dearly beloved in Christ, what is your request?

   ALL: We ask your blessing, Father, for we acknowledge that we are sinners and we wish to renew our conversion to the Lord in and before His Holy Church.

   PRIEST: May the Lord be in your hearts and on your lips. May He fill you with faith, hope and love. May He give you a true spirit of repentance and grant you the courage to properly confess all of your sins in the name of the Father and of the Son and of the Holy Spirit.

ALL: Amen.

PRIEST: Let us all pray the first part of "I confess."

ALL: I confess to Almighty God/ to blessed Mary ever Virgin,/ to blessed Michael the archangel/ to blessed John the Baptist/ to the holy apostles, Peter and Paul/ to all the saints/ to you, Father/ and to all of these here present/ joined with me in this celebration of the sacrament of reconciliation/ that I have sinned exceedingly in thought, word and deed./ Through my fault,/ through my fault/ through my most grievous fault.

PRIEST: Please be seated now for the public examination of conscience. The commentator will help direct your thoughts to the words of Christ and suggest points for your examination.

6. Here a commentator will suggest the points of examination. This is optional but recommended. In the following appendix, you will find a suggested list of examination for adults and children.

7. After the examination is over, there should be a short time of personal prayer and meditation. After that the Priest will say:

8. PRIEST: Let us all now kneel and conclude the "I confess."

ALL: Therefore, I beseech blessed Mary ever Virgin/ blessed Michael the archangel/ blessed John the Baptist/ the holy apostles Peter and Paul/ all the saints/ you, Father/ and those of you gathered here with me/ to pray to the Lord our God for me.

PRIEST: May Almighty God have mercy on you, forgive you your sins and bring you to life everlasting.

ALL: Amen.

PRIEST: May the Almighty and merciful Lord grant you pardon, absolution and remission of all your sins.

ALL: Amen.

9. The priest makes an announcement here that the confessional part of the sacrament will take place. He urges the people to enter the confessional and make their confession the usual way or any way that they think expresses themselves and their sorrow. He may remind the people that the absolution following applies only to those who have confessed grave sin in the confessional and those with venial sins. It does not apply to those in grave sin who do not go to confession. A sufficient number of priests should be available, of course, to make the procedure comfortable. The priests may choose not to give the penance and absolution in the confessional. These are recommended to be done outside together. In some cases, the priests will go to confession first to one another as a moving part of the service. While the private confessions are being heard, the others may either pray in silence or recite one of the penitential psalms.

10. After all are reassembled, the priests involved all come together and give absolution in unison. Then the priest says: "Again we emphasize the communal aspects of this celebration by saying our penance in common. Let us remember that the liturgical penance of the sacrament is a sign of the total reparation we owe to God's love for our own sins and those of the entire world." There is now recited a common penance. Psalm 50 is highly recommended. In addition to the recitation of some prayers, the priest may give some good action to do.

11. After the penance, there may be some dialogue petitions as follows:

PRIEST: Now please stand for the following petitions and responses:
"That we may embrace the spirit of Christian penance in our personal lives . . . let us pray to the Lord!"

ALL: Lord, let us believe your words that we must all do penance lest we perish.

PRIEST: "That we may demonstrate our love for the Lord by loving one another as He has loved us . . . let us pray to the Lord!"

ALL: Lord, grant us the spirit of charity, fellowship and true brotherhood.

PRIEST: "That by being more concerned about others in our work and activities than ourselves, we may deny our selfish satisfactions . . . let us pray to the Lord!"

ALL: Lord, may the spirit of your love urge us on to the service of others.

PRIEST: Almighty Father and friend, our God, who at our baptism gave us a special bond of friendship in the Holy Spirit and have just restored this friendship with us, may the sprinkling of this blessed water be for all of us here a reminder of our commitment at baptism, a pledge of everlasting life, of peace and joy through Jesus Christ our Lord.

ALL: Amen.

12. Here the priest tells the people to kneel while he goes up and down the aisle sprinkling them with holy water. After this is done, he says aloud to them:

PRIEST: May the passion of Our Lord Jesus Christ, the merits of the blessed Virgin Mary and of all the saints, and also whatever good you do in your life or whatever hardship you endure, be for you the cause of the remission of your sins, the increase of grace and the reward of everlasting life.

ALL: Amen.

13. At this point there may be some physical sign of unity and fellowship. Recommended are the handshake of peace or simply silently all holding hands for a moment. After this the recessional takes place the same way as the processional. All exit singing some happy song such as "Allelu!"

Such is a basic format of a communal confession:

1. entrance hymn
2. prayer
3. Scripture reading
4. homily
5. the confiteor
6. examination of conscience
7. private confessions
8. absolution in unison
9. public recitation of penance
10. litany
11. sprinkling with holy water
12. exit hymn

These steps may be omitted or rearranged. Likewise different themes for the different parts of the liturgical year can be arranged. In any case, it would be well for the priest and a committee to go over the format first and be sure that a copy is mimeographed for each participant. This sample can be quite successfully adapted for children. The use of the communal confession is to be especially recommended at least twice a year before Christmas and Easter. A few explanatory talks in preparation will be especially rewarding.

APPENDIX II

Suggested Examination of Conscience

There are two examinations of conscience given here. One is for children, the other for adults. It should be obvious that another person cannot examine someone else's conscience. On the other hand, the broad areas that might otherwise be missed can be offered for consideration. Thus, these examinations are not so explicit as they are general, suggesting wide patterns of thought and broad patterns of attitude. There are several pamphlets that do give rather detailed examinations. For example there's a pamphlet called "Examination of Conscience for Married Couples," by Edwin Haungs, S. J. put out by Liguorian Pamphlets, Liguori, Missouri. There's a good examination translated from the French that is telling in its raising of social commitments for the Christian. It is called "Examination of Conscience for Adults," and is written by L. J. Lebret and T. Suavet.

What follows then, is one man's suggestions of broad outlines trying to cover the areas of vocation, charity and ommission suggested in the book.

A. Examination of Conscience for Children

1. What is my attitude towards my vocation as a student?
2. Do I give the study to my work as I am obliged to?
3. Am I faithful in doing my homework?
4. Do I copy another's work and thus steal another's knowledge and labor?
5. Do I cheat on tests?
6. What do I contribute to the class spirit?
7. Do I raise my hand, ask questions?
8. Do I take time out to help another in school work?
9. What do I really think of my classmates?
10. Am I aware that the dumbest, the most unpopular may be the closest to God?
11. How do I treat the boy or girl I dislike so much? Do I at least pray for them?
12. Do I snub or ignore the kid I don't like?
13. Do I repeat dirty stories and jokes and so hurt my friends?
14. What's my conduct in the school yard?
15. Do I bully or over-tease other kids?
16. Do I cheat in games?
17. Do I help out at home—and without always being asked?
18. How do I treat my brothers and sisters?
19. Do I ever volunteer to do an act of charity for my parents?
20. Do I make fun of other kids, "cut them up"?
21. What have I left undone that I ought to do?
22. Do I fail to be kind to another because of pressure?
23. Am I afraid to walk away from the bad story?
24. What have I done for the poor? do I ever put anything in the poor box?
25. Do I ever think of the kids my age in the orphanage, in Vietnam?
26. Have I prayed? especially in time of temptation?
27. Do I miss Mass which is the community worship of God?
28. Do I ever think of Jesus during the day? Drop into church?

29. Do I make fun of another's nationality, color, defects?
30. Do I really try to show good examples?
31. What have I done recently to make my friends holier?
32. Do I realize that I and my brothers and sisters form one community, one People of God?
33. Am I aware that my sins have offended the 'whole Christ' and that is why I am here now in front of everybody examining my conscience?
34. Am I about to approach Christ in the sacrament of reconciliation with faith?
35. With joy and happiness?
36. With confidence like the Prodigal Son returning home?
37. Am I looking for an "instant cure" or do I realize that my friendship with Jesus, like all friendships, must take time to grow?
38. Am I about to give the priest time to talk to me, help me?
39. Finally, do I really realize that Jesus is here among us and so very happy at what we are doing?

B. EXAMINATION OF CONSCIENCE FOR ADULTS

1. What have I done to make our marriage grow?
2. Have I been thoughtful of my partner?
3. Have I been so interested in my work or hobby that I've neglected the other?
4. Have my children become so preoccupying that I have not given proper effort to our married love?
5. Have I been peevish and spiteful towards my spouse?
•6. What has been my example to my children?
7. Do we pray ever as a family?
8. Do we have little liturgical celebrations in our home?
9. When was the last time I said the magic words, "I love you"?
10. Have I contributed to my parish in any way?
11. Have I had the courage to disagree with my pastor or offer my aid?

12. Do I know my fellow parishioners, my fellow members of the Mystical Body?
13. Have I made an effort to get to know them?
14. Do I just criticize or am I willing to help out?
15. Have I ever thought about my parish and what is best for it or am I just leaving it to others?
16. What are my community needs?
17. Am I aware of any poor people? where they live? who they are?
18. Did I speak up when the conversation was getting bad?
19. Did I make an effort to speak to the neighbor who is a boor and whom everyone else shuns?
20. Have I passed on my prejudices to my children?
21. Was I too lazy to help my partner?
22. Was I too preoccupied with my own petty problems not to see the ache in the heart of another?
23. Do I take part in the Liturgy—even if I don't like it?
24. Am I "too busy" for my children?
25. Do I make a conscious effort to see Christ in all?
26. How do I do my job? indifferently? with a sense of vocation?
27. What have I left undone?
28. Am I still bearing grudges?
29. Am I aware that Christianity is a religion of service?
30. In readying for confession, where is my emphasis: on me or on Christ?
31. Do I realize that going to confession is "liturgy"?
32. Am I bringing faith to this encounter with Christ?
33. Do I realize that I am confessing to the Whole Christ; that is, to all my brothers in Christ as well?
34. Am I ready with faith?
35. Am I sorry that I can't be sorry?

APPENDIX III

A Selected Bibliography

As indicated in the introduction there are many fine books on the different aspects of sin, repentance and confession. They range from the very scholarly to the popular. Here is a list of books and articles which the interested reader may pursue if he wishes. I have added comments to guide the reader as to the difficulty of the books involved.

Betz, Otto, editor, *Making Sense of Confession*, Franciscan Herald Press, Chicago, 1968. Very easy and rewarding reading. Concentrates on the preparation of children for confession.

Buckley, Francis J., S.J. "What Age for First Confession?" *Irish Ecclesiastical Record* (April 1967) pp. 221-52. Readable survey on self-explanatory subject.

Concilium, "Moral Problems and Christian Personalism," Vol. 5 in the Moral Theology Series, Paulist Press, Glen Rock, N.J. 1965. Essays for the scholar.

Connell, F. J., C.S.S.R., "First Communion Without Confession," *American Ecclesiastical Review*, 151 (1964) pp. 267-69.

Cooke, Bernard J., *Christian Sacraments and Christian Personality*, Holt, Rinehart and Winston, New York, 1965. Definitely some theological background needed to understand this excellent book.

Corrigan, John E., "Bless Me, Father." A pamphlet put out by Claretian Publications, 221 West Madison St., Chicago, Illinois, 60606. Good pamphlet on a more in-depth approach to examination of conscience.

Coudreau, F., *Catechesis and Sin*, Macmillan, New York, 1962. Good reading.

Curran, Charles E., *A New Look at Christian Morality*, Fides, Notre Dame, Indiana, 1968. A series of formerly printed essays on various aspects of morality. New and interesting approach on present day moral questions. See also his essay on penance in *Contemporary Problems in Moral Theology*, Fides, 1970.

Evely, Louis, *That Man is You*, The Newman Press, Westminster, Maryland, 1964. Scattered through this and the other books of Father Evely are wonderful insights and spiritual approaches to confession. All of his books are highly recommended.

Gesell, A., Ilg, Frances, and Ames, Louis, *Youth: the Years From Ten to Sixteen*, Harper, 1956. Part of their exhaustive series on children's development. Well done and easy to read.

Haring, Bernard, *Shalom: Peace*, Farrar, Straus and Giroux, New York, 1967. Good and readable general survey of moral questions. A kind of moral theology textbook.

Heggen, F. J., *Confession and the Service of Penance:* University of Notre Dame Press, Notre Dame, Indiana, 1968. Requires close reading. Good.

Killgallon and Weber, *We Live in Union with God's Family*, Benziger Brothers, New York, 1968. The author's new book for children in preparing them for first confession. A school text book that parents will benefit from.

Killgallon and Weber, *Beyond the Commandments*. Herder and Herder, New York, New York, 1965. These two Chicago priests have done consistently wonderful work in translating Vatican II and general theology to the masses. Good and recommended reading on general approach and attitude towards morality.

Leenan, James, O.S.C., "Penance and Its Social Dimensions" *Homiletic and Pastoral Review*, 68 (1968) pp. 494-502. Good insight into community aspects of sin.

Monden, Louis, S.J., *Sin, Liberty and Law*, Sheed and Ward, New York, 1965. Again, this wonderful book is not easy reading for the uninitiated, but it is well worth the effort.

A New Catechism, Herder and Herder, New York, 1967. This new catechism for adults does a fine job on the whole question of sin and repentance.

O'Callaghan, Denis, editor, *Sin and Repentance*, Alba House, Staten Island, New York, 1967. A series of papers from Ireland on the different aspects of sin and confession. Readable.

O'Neil, Robert P., and Donovan, Michael A., "Psychological Development and the Concept of Mortal Sin." *Insight* (Fall, 1965) pp. 1-7 and *"The Question of Preadolescent Sin,"* *Insight* (Spring, 1966), pp. 1-10. Both good investigations into the theological and psychological abilities of children to sin.

Piaget, J., *The Moral Judgment of the Child*, Free Press, Glencoe, Illinois, 1948. The famous Swiss psychologist findings in this field. Technical.

Poschmann, B., *Penance and the Anointing of the Sick*, Herder & Herder, New York, 1964. A classic work on the subjects; definitely scholarly.

Rahner, Karl, S.J., *Theological Investigations*, Volumes II and III. Helicon Press, Baltimore, 1967. These two volumes contain various essays on confession. Father Rahner always writes well and lucidly when treating spiritual subjects. These essays are interesting and valuable.

Riga, Peter, *Sin and Penance*, Bruce, Milwaukee, 1961. Theologically oriented but not difficult. Good selection on history of confession.

Ruef, John J., C.S.S.R., "The Age for First Confession" *ibid.* pp. 503-510. The author takes an opposite view of the advocates of changing children's confessions until they are older. Well done.

Sherrin, John, C.S.P., *The Sacrament of Freedom*, Bruce, Milwaukee, 1960. Popular and somewhat dated treatment of the sacrament.

Sloyan, Gerald, *How Do I Know I'm Doing Right?* Pflaum, Dayton, Ohio, 1966. Good and popular explanation of conscience and morality.

Uleyn, Arnold, *Is It I, Lord?* Holt, Rinehart and Winston, New York, 1969. A priest psychiatrist looks at sin, guilt and repentance. Well done if somewhat technical for the average reader.

APPENDIX IV

Discussion Starters
for Study Groups

MEETING ONE

Chapter One: Friendship

1. How is your relationship with a friend different from your relationship with anyone else?
2. What are the implications of the statement, "God is our Friend"?
3. Why should we first teach children that God is a loving Father before we speak to them of sin?
4. Why is there danger in thinking of sin as a "thing" or a "quantity"?
5. What does the word, "grace" have to do with our relationship with God?

Chapter Two: Sin

1. What is sin?
2. Would you use the terms, "grave" and "venial" when teaching your child about sin? Why or why not?

3. What is the difference between doing wrong and committing sin?
4. Do you agree with the author's statement that: "a healthy sense of sin" is the beginning of salvation?

Meeting Two

Chapter Three: Christian Morality

1. In what way did Jesus add a whole new dimension to Old Testament Morality?
2. What is it that forms the basis of Jesus' teaching on morality?
3. What approach would you use in teaching children the ten commandments?
4. What do you think St. Paul meant by the statement, "For if you are led by the Spirit, you are not under the Law"?
5. Jesus denounced the "pharisaism" of his day. Do you think there is a certain amount of "pharisaism" present in those who are his followers today?

Chapter Four: The New Morality

1. What is the essential difference between "the new morality" and the "old morality"?
2. Do you agree with the familiar quotation, "You have to love your neighbor, but you don't have to like him?"
3. What is your reaction to the "fish-mass-sex" summary of morality as opposed to the new morality of "social responsibility"?
4. How would you answer an adolescent who asks, "How far can I go before it's a sin" in sexual behavior?
5. How can a person be sorry for a sin which brought him pleasure?

Meeting Three

Chapter Five: The Over-All Record

1. What do theologians understand by the term, "fundamental option"?
2. Do you agree that God judges a person "not on a single act, but on his over-all record?"
3. Do you think that the "over-all record" concept minimizes the seriousness of sin?
4. What is the difference between "grave sins" and "mortal sin"?
5. Can a mortal sin be isolated from the acts which have led up to it?

Chapter Six: Conscience

1. What is conscience?
2. In what way is it true to say that children "inherit conscience"?
3. Do you see any danger in the statement, "follow your own conscience"?
4. What do you understand by the term, "moral schizophrenia"?
5. Give concrete examples of how parents can help their child develop a positive attitude toward God rather than a legalistic attitude toward Him.

Meeting Four

Chapter Seven: Signs and Faith

1. Why is it so important that we, as Catholics, understand the meaning and function of signs?
2. What do the Gospels tell us about Jesus' attitude toward sinners?
3. Why tell your sins to a priest?

4. The sacraments "work automatically." What is true and what is false about this statement?

5. How would you explain the Sacrament of Penance to your child?

Chapter Eight: Sin and Community

1. What are the full implications of Jesus' statement: "I am the Vine, you are the branches"?

2. How does one person's sin affect the whole family of God?

3. What did the term, "ex-communication," mean to the members of the early Church?

4. Why is it significant that the penitents of the early Church were received "back into the Church" on Holy Thursday?

MEETING FIVE

Chapter Nine: A Brief History of Confession

1. Why was there no explicit reference to confession before the third or fourth centuries?

2. In what way would you consider the disciplinary practices of the third and fourth centuries to be "harsh"?

3. How did the Sacrament of Penance come to be associated with death in the early centuries of the church?

4. How did the "Irish Monks" of the seventh and eighth centuries bring about a change of attitude toward the Sacrament of Penance?

Chapter Ten: First Confession for Children

1. What is the distinction between "material" and "formal" wrong?

2. Why is it not necessary for children to go to confession before receiving First Holy Communion?

3. What are some of the reasons for postponing the age of first confession?

4. What would you say to a person who argues that children should "get into the habit of going to confession at an early age"?

MEETING SIX

Chapter Eleven: Formula and Examination
1. What are the full implications of the word, "bless," as used in the confession formula?
2. What, to you, seems to be the most meaningful kind of penance that the priest could give?
3. Do you go along with the idea of having a "regular confessor"?
4. What would you say to a person who argues that "Confession doesn't do me any good, so I don't go anymore"?
5. In the light of what you have read in this chapter, do you think your next confession will be different?

Chapter Twelve: It is the Lord!
1. With what attitudes should we approach the Lord in the Sacrament of Penance?
2. Where should the emphasis be in the liturgy of the Sacrament of Penance?
3. How are we like the Prodigal Son?
4. What does the story of the Prodigal Son teach us about God the Father?
5. How is the story of the Prodigal Son a summary of the twelve chapters of this book?

MEETING SEVEN

It is suggested that a communal penance celebration be held for the members of the group.